THE TRAGEDY OF STATE

First published in 1971 by
Methuen & Co. Ltd
11 New Fetter Lane, London EC4P 4EE
Reprinted with new introduction 1987

Published in the USA by
Methuen & Co.
in association with Methuen, Inc.
29 West 35th Street, New York, NY 10001

British Library Cataloguing in Publication Data
Lever, J.W.
The tragedy of state: a study of Jacobean drama.
1. English drama (Tragedy) – History and criticism
2. English drama – 17th century – History and criticism
3. English drama – Early modern and Elizabethan, 1500-1600
– History and criticism
I. Title
822'. 0512' 09   PR658.T7
ISBN 0 - 416 - 70000 - 4

Library of Congress Cataloging in Publication Data
Lever, J.W. (Julius Walter)
The tragedy of state.
Bibliography: p.
Includes index.
1. English drama – 17th century – History and criticism.
2. English drama (Tragedy) – History and criticism.
3. Politics in literature.
I. Title
PR678.P65L48   1987   822'.3'09358   87-5744
ISBN 0 - 416 - 70000 - 4 (pbk.)

Contents

Introduction

According to one view of the appropriate credentials for writing this kind of introduction I perhaps shouldn't be doing it. J. W. Lever and I didn't share the same university or colleagues; he wasn't my mentor, nor was I taught by him; I didn't attend his lectures or even know him at a distance. So this isn't – and couldn't be – an academic encomium presupposing any of that. But I can write as someone who was inspired by *The Tragedy of State* when I came across it by chance as a student; who returned to it often and rewardingly when later writing about the drama of the period; who has seen other, more recent, generations of students engaging enthusiastically with it. This introduction is meant for such students: it aims to sketch briefly some of the larger critical, intellectual, aesthetic and political issues which concerned Lever and which remain current within contemporary cultural criticism and literary theory; additionally the accompanying references are offered as a guide to further reading.

Lever announces in his preface his intention to consider Jacobean tragedy as radically engaged with contemporary political issues. In this, he continues, he went against prevailing criticism and scholarship which wanted to see the dramatists as pillars of orthodoxy 'affirming concepts of "order and degree" which opposed any major political or social change' – this was the so-called Elizabethan World Picture or Order (pp. xix and 5).

Much subsequent criticism and scholarship has sided with Lever. The view which he saw as prevailing then is no longer dominant. Certainly it no longer needs refuting. Lever didn't devote a great deal of space to refuting it even then, but what he did say about the Elizabethan World Order was provocative: 'Corresponding to nothing in the experience or speculative thought of the age, this creed of absolutism served chiefly to bolster up a precarious monarchy which lacked a standing army or an efficient police force.' (p. 5)

By no means all critics before Lever subscribed to the orthodox view. And anyway it is misleading to think of critical opinion as being simply correct or incorrect in its interpretation of specific works or, more generally, a body of literature. Critical positions are often culturally revealing in their own right, even (or indeed especially) when they are no longer dominant. Moreover, understood in this way, we can find continuities between one critical position and those coexisting with or actually opposed to it, or even those which claim to supersede it.

One such continuity in English Studies, and of especial relevance to tragedy, is the view of great literature as affirming psychic or spiritual transcendence. Of course conflict, failure and disorder are the stuff of literature, as they are of history and life itself. But it is the overcoming, the transcendence of these things that matters. The so-called Elizabethan World Picture was only ever a particular and perhaps facile version of this view, which I call idealist as opposed to materialist, the latter position being outlined in what follows.[1] Idealist criticism constitutes a longer, more pervasive, complex and demanding tradition than that represented by those who wanted to reimagine the Elizabethan World Picture. To understand that tradition better we might return to a famous observation by Marx on the dual nature of religion as he saw it:

> *Religious* suffering is at the same time an expression of real suffering and a *protest* against real suffering. Religion is the sigh of the oppressed creature, the sentiment of a heartless world, and the soul of soulless conditions. It is the *opium* of the people.
>
> The abolition of religion, as the *illusory* happiness of men, is a demand for their *real* happiness. The call to abandon their illusions about their condition is a *call to abandon a condition which requires illusions.*[2]

On the one hand then religion can be seen as a form of mystification, most especially perhaps in the way it locates the causes of suffering in the realm of the unalterable – fate, God, the human condition – with the consequence that suffering is inevitable and must be endured. And suffering further promises to become the grounds of tragic knowledge, of spiritual redemption and perhaps finally of transcendence, the transformation in and of death itself. Man learns wisdom through suffering. On the other hand, even if the realm of religious compensation is an illusion, the very need for that compensation could be seen as an *implicit* protest against suffering. Oscar Wilde, in his essay on socialism, offered an interesting elaboration of this argument. He observed that 'the Ideals that we owe to Christ are the ideals of the man who abandons society entirely, or of the man who resists society absolutely. But man is naturally social'.[3] The Christian antithesis of the social, the realm of the spirit, is also the real of pain as an ideal medium of self-realization. For most of us though the reality of suffering is very different.

In an important essay, 'The Affirmative Character of Culture', Herbert Marcuse showed how the contradictory nature of religion is carried over into bourgeois culture, and especially its art. And, we might add, into some literary criticism. Idealist criticism similarly creates an ideal perspective – aesthetic, ethical, spiritual – which both compensates for, and mystifies, the actual suffering and misery that figures so prominently in life and art. At the same time this ideal perspective registers the need for a better existence than the one actually available.[4] Marcuse's article begs important distinctions; for example, neither art nor bourgeois culture should be treated as unitary. But its central contention – that art and culture inherit from religion a contradictory position which simultaneously mystifies and registers suffering, submits to and yet (implicitly at least) protests against it – suggests a way of understanding a significant tradition within English Studies, and in particular its concern with tragedy and the Renaissance, the period when tragedy is said to have had its greatest flourishing.

Idealist criticism has often been explicitly Christian in perspective. And, even where it has drawn back from the doctrinal perspective of Christianity, or been actively sceptical of Christianity or indeed anti-Christian, its language has often remained religiose, especially in the acceptance of suffering as inescapable yet mysteriously ennobling, redemptive even. In a book influential in the decade preceding the first appearance of Lever's *Tragedy of State*, George Steiner eloquently insisted:

> in the very excess of his suffering lies man's claim to dignity. Powerless and broken . . . he assumes a new grandeur. Man is ennobled by the vengeful spite or injustice of the gods. . . . Hence there is in the final moments of great tragedy, whether Greek, or Shakespearean, or neoclassic, a fusion of grief and joy, of lament over the fall of man and of rejoicing in the resurrection of his spirit. No other poetic form achieves this mysterious effect; it makes of *Oedipus*, *King Lear*, and *Phedre* the noblest yet wrought by the mind.[5]

Within literary criticism we can of course trace this view back to A. C. Bradley's *Shakespearean Tragedy*, a classic working out of the idealist theory which cautiously broke with the Christian metaphysic.[6] Steiner breaks with it much more emphatically by saying that as Christianity believes in an ultimate justice, where there is justice there cannot be tragedy (pp. 6, 324, 331). Even so, the idealist reading of tragedy, especially Steiner's, is inescapably rooted in religion and we therefore find its most cogent expression not in the diluted religiosity of literary criticism, within which literature has often been a substitute or compromise theology, but in the work of those who remain confidently committed to its metaphysical origins. I have

[ix]

in mind especially *Beyond Tragedy*, an important work by the Protestant theologian Reinhold Niebuhr.[7] In a chapter entitled 'Christianity and Tragedy' he gives a bold summary of the idealist preoccupation with integrity, subjectivity and suffering:

> In true tragedy the hero defies malignant power to assert the integrity of his soul. . . . The really tragic hero of warfare is not the soldier who makes the greatest sacrifice but the occasional discerning spirit who plunges into the chaos of war with a full understanding of its dark, unconscious sources in the human psyche and an equal resolution, either to defy these forces or to submit himself as their tool and victim in recognition of his common humanity with those who are unconscious victims. (pp. 156, 158).

Even those advocates of the tragic vision who argue that Christianity is finally incompatible with it, would probably go this far with Niebuhr. So while there are important differences between Bradley, Niebuhr and Steiner, they share an equally important perception of tragedy as focusing profound and ennobling truths about the human condition in the suffering integrity of the unique individual.

In *The Tragedy of State* Lever largely breaks with this long and influential tradition. He sees the protagonists of Jacobean drama differently: 'we are not greatly concerned with the characters as individuals . . . in Jacobean tragedy it is not primarily the conduct of the individual, but of the society which assails him, that stands condemned' (pp. 10, 12; cf. p. 13). Of John Webster's play by the same name, he says 'The White Devil is not Vittoria Corombona but Renaissance Europe' (p. 86); of Bosola, the malcontent in Webster's other major play, *The Duchess of Malfi*, he says 'Neither villain nor hero, Bosola typifies the plight of the intellectual in the world of state, at once its agent and victim.' (p. 94) Lever's argument here is most immediately with those who saw the plays as growing out of the medieval morality tradition and working as exemplary warnings of God's retribution on those who transgress. But Lever is also offering a materialist alternative to the more searching idealist perspective of those like Niebuhr and Steiner. Many of the differences between the idealist and the materialist perspectives centre, as here, on opposed conceptions of individuality and subjectivity. I shall return to this, but before moving on we should note that Lever retains a concern for suffering integrity, especially when it occurs in the form of stoic rationality, which he sees as a strong influence on the drama (see for example pp. 10 and 94). At the same time he believes that a play which shows the defeat and destruction of human integrity does not thereby cease to be tragic (p. 10).

[x]

Another dispute concerns the relationship of the social and the political to the tragic: in effect, what counts as tragic? Steiner is emphatic:

> The tragic personage is broken by forces which can neither be fully understood nor overcome by rational prudence. This again is crucial. Where the causes of disaster are temporal, where the conflict can be resolved through technical or social means, we may have serious drama, but not tragedy. . . . The distinction should be borne sharply in mind. Tragedy is irreparable.   (p.8)

In a sense then Lever's tragedy of state is what Steiner says tragedy cannot be. It isn't that Lever sees Jacobean tragedy as politically optimistic, rather that, in contradistinction to Steiner, he sees the causes of suffering and conflict in these tragedies as contingent rather than necessary, and the effect of social and historical forces focused in state power. Though terrifyingly destructive, these forces are not irresistible in the sense of being cosmically or divinely destined. Again, we can compare with Steiner: 'In Greek tragedy, as in Shakespeare, mortal actions are encompassed by forces which transcend man' (p. 193); '"authentic tragedy" presupposes hell' (p. 128).

Lever's book appeared in 1971, just one decade after Steiner's. That decade was a notoriously eventful one, not least with respect to the political radicalism of many young people. It is hard to believe that any intellectual (or even academic) could have remained unaffected by the radicalism of that decade (if only to oppose it), although the work of some literary critics suggests that they did. Lever's book originated not as a monograph for other scholars and critics but as a series of lectures for students. Not surprisingly then, he begins with a question that had become almost unavoidable after the student radicalism of the previous few years – and this is the question of relevance, to which he has an unambiguous answer:

> In the present-day world, alienated in poverty and affluence, dehumanised by state bureaucracies and military machines, the most urgent study of mankind would seem to be not the eternal human condition, but the prospect of survival in the face of impersonal power drives.   (p. 1)

Lever registers an intellectual and political commitment that was rare among literary critics at that time. One response of the teacher to the question about relevance was simply to dismiss it as irrelevant to the study of literature; another was to see that question as the consequence of narrow-minded ignorance which only impartial teaching would rectify (as the unfortunate (though fortunately unrepresentative) motto of my own university has it: 'Be still and know' or, as it is sometimes glossed, 'Shut up and think what you're told').

The patronizing review of Lever's *The Tragedy of State* in *The Times Literary Supplement* of 17 December 1971 says a great deal:

> It seems unfortunate that this constant and often unavailing search for 'relevance' should occupy so many pages of this study since, when Mr Lever can escape from its entanglements he shows himself a sound and often subtle expositor. His treatment of theme and character is penetrating, and we must regret that his preoccupation with real or supposed political features causes him at times to neglect the play's dramatic qualities. (p. 1583 unsigned, according to the convention at that time.)

To reject the terms and implied perspective of this review is not necessarily to remain uncritical of the concept of relevance. Like many other indispensable concepts it can be ambiguous and open to several conflicting interpretations. Historically – meaning at that time and in relation to the institutions within which it was made – the student demand for relevance was a political demand. And, for the materialist perspective outlined here, a progressive one also. Even so it could be used in the name of a certain myopia (the demand for relevance sliding into one for sameness, 'relevant to' into 'same as') and so entail a disregard of cultural difference, both past and present. And yet it was the very demand for relevance which helped produce the recognition of its limitations and the need to address questions of cultural and historical difference. This tension (between relevance and difference) itself helped shift English Studies in the direction of a wider ranging cultural politics and interdisciplinary intellectual concern, with implications at once methodological, political and ethical.[8]

Not for Lever then the human condition, nor merely that 'treatment of theme and character' which the *TLS* reviewer wished he'd stuck to, but rather a criticism that explores the Jacobean dramatists' own concern with state power in a period of 'intellectual ferment and spiritual upheaval which preceded the first great European revolution' (p. xix). This particular aspect of Lever's project found confirmation outside literary criticism. In two recent articles Christopher Hill offers a persuasive synthesis of the evidence for not just seeing contemporary politics as a recurring concern, but also the wider significance of the drama for understanding subsequent history. Writers of literature, especially drama, were, says Hill, 'not dealing with "the human condition", with "man", but with specific problems which confronted rulers and their subjects in a specific historical situation – problems which were bloodily resolved in the sixteen-forties'.[9]

Another historian, Lawrence Stone, has provided a framework for understanding the longer-term implications of literature and politics. He has argued, for example, that the important issue is not so much war breaking out in 1642 but why established institutions of the state and the church – crown, court, central administration, army and episcopacy – collapsed in the period leading up to that event.[10] One contributory factor was surely a theatre in which these institutions, together with their ideological legitimation, were subjected to sceptical and hostile representations. Strikingly, Franco Moretti makes Elizabethan and Jacobean tragedy a major exception to his general theory of literature as a conservative form, which tends to secure consent to (because it is an ideological legitimation of) the existing order. Moretti argues that it 'contributed, more radically than any other cultural phenomenon of the same period, to discrediting the values of absolute monarchy, thereby paving the way, with wholly destructive means, for the English Revolution'. Here Moretti stresses, as others have recently, the revolutionary political potential of negation: tragedy, in this period, was 'an unrivalled instrument of criticism and dissent'. Shakespeare may announce the dawn of bourgeois civilization, but not by prefiguring it. On the contrary, he demonstrates inexorably how, obeying the old rules, which are the only ones he knows, the world can only fall apart.[11]

Lever's concern with state power remains of course a concern for us today. But since the appearance of *The Tragedy of State* a range of different, but often related perspectives, has transformed our understanding of the operations of power at other levels as well, especially in the formation of class and sexual identity, of subjectivity and gender relations, by which I mean the diverse perspectives within feminism, post-structuralism, psychoanalysis and materialism. All of these have had an influence on Renaissance studies, so much so in fact that there is not room here to indicate the full extent of that influence, even for Jacobean drama.[12] Some of these perspectives involve formidable intellectual difficulty. Undoubtedly this is often the necessary consequence of radically new ways of thinking. But it can also be the consequence of a specious and obscurantist complexity. The situation is complicated by the fact that sometimes those who have brought the charge of obscurantism themselves subscribe to a complacent common sense and anti-intellectualism which has been visible too often in English Studies. Lever's book, as already pointed out, originated as student lectures and, as such, is a model of that clarity derived not from anti-intellectualism but, on the contrary, from a real intellectual integrity.

One development that has arisen from these perspectives concentrates upon oppression and exploitation of the marginal, the subordinate and the

[xiii]

excluded (something already apparent in Lever's study). It is not of course that the awareness of such things has only just occurred or that they relate only to minorities; how could they, historically, in the case of the subordinate classes, women or Third World countries subjected to an imperialist rule? At this point the *TLS* reviewer might object that this has nothing to do with Jacobean drama, and once again we have drifted into a misguided concern for relevance. On the contrary, issues of class, sexuality, imperialist and colonial exploitation have everything to do with Jacobean drama, as recent studies have made abundantly clear.[13]

Another important consequence of the study of power has been to reveal that those areas of human life commonly thought to be antithetical to and independent of the political realm – for example subjectivity, personal identity, gender identity, the privacy of the home or the intimacy of the family – in fact not only correlate with, but actively reproduce the exploitation, repression and oppression that is obviously visible in that larger realm. And some modes of oppression, for example patriarchy, phallocentrism and misogyny in the case of the oppression of women, are of course internalized psychically as well as working institutionally and legally.[14] This has considerable importance for the drama, not just because patriarchy and misogyny pervade it, but because this is a drama in which we see these things operating at all levels – the psychic, the private, the familial, the public.

So we arrive back at issues of individual subjectivity, though now with a perspective far removed from the *TLS* reviewer's concern with theme and character, or Steiner's concern with the tragic subject (essential self) and 'his' exemplification of 'Man' and the human condition. Within this different perspective and indeed within Jacobean tragedy, the human subject is seen not as the antithesis of the social and the political, but as their focus. Sometimes this is put more provocatively: far from being the origin of the social and the political, subjectivity is actually one of their effects, hence the frequently observed linguistic link between subjectivity and subjection. The idea here is that we more effectively conform to a dominant order if we have internalized its values as part of our identity rather than if that order has continually to coerce us into conformity. So, for example, to the extent that we have internalized our respective identities as 'masculine' or 'feminine', we perpetuate unawares an entire social order which depends on that rigid opposition, frequently oppressively of course.[15] The irony is that often, when we think we are being 'naturally' and freely ourselves – as opposed to playing this or that particular social role – the reverse is actually the case.

[xiv]

Returning now to the different theories of tragedy and the part which the individual plays in each, we are in a position to see the force of one of Marx's most famous formulations of his philosophy (the sixth thesis on Feuerbach): 'Feuerbach resolves the essence of religion into the essence of *man*. But the essence is not an abstraction inherent in each particular individual. The real nature of man is the totality of social relations'.[16] Arguably, in *The Death of Tragedy* Steiner also resolves the essence of religion into the essence of 'man.' Marx's alternative view, which stresses the social construction of identity, and finds some kind of endorsement in the various kinds of literary theory, might well seem to contradict some of the central assumptions of traditional English Studies.

Recently, writing from within South Africa, Martin Orkin has shown how the idealist theory of tragedy, and especially that of Shakespearean tragedy, colludes ideologically with the aims of the dominant order in that country. Whereas much South African drama has been marginalized or banned, Shakespeare continues to figure centrally in a conservatively governed education system. As Orkin shows in his important critique, this is predominantly an idealist Shakespeare concerned with the suffering and integrity of the individual and supposedly transhistorical truths about a human nature – I use 'supposedly' because these truths are usually and obviously culturally specific.[17] I am aware that, to finish by gesturing towards the South African situation, is to be open to the charge of easy moralism. This would indeed be so if I thought that our own culture was innocent (culturally) of complicity with what is happening there. Manifestly it is not, the origins of South Africa's Shakespeare are here. Moreover, the same essentially conservative and often reactionary use of Shakespeare continues to occur within our own culture. The evidence for this is more than conclusive.[18] Of course there are differences and it is necessary to insist on these too. But it is usually the case that those differences are complacently assumed to be so considerable as to disqualify the comparison I am suggesting. Recent work on the reproduction of Shakespeare proves otherwise; it points to structural similarities. In both cultures the 'truths' of the human condition, profound precisely because they transcend politics, in fact typically help to legitimate conservative politics. This fact has been recognized for some time, and is observed by several of the writers mentioned including Marx, Wilde, Marcuse and, of course, Lever himself: it is surely why on page one of this book he directs us towards the tragedy of state and not that of 'the eternal human condition'.

NOTES

1. For a fuller account of both see J. Dollimore, *Radical Tragedy: Religion Ideology and Power in the Drama of Shakespeare and his Contemporaries*, Brighton: Harvester, 1984, esp. pp. 49–50, 53–6, 156–8, 189–95.

2. Karl Marx, *Early Writings*, ed. T. B. Bottomore, London: Watts, 1963, pp. 43-4.

3. Oscar Wilde, 'The Soul of Man Under Socialism', in *The Artist as Critic: Critical Writings of Oscar Wilde*. ed. Richard Ellmann, London: W. H. Allen, 1970, pp. 255–89.

4. Herbert Marcuse, 'The Affirmative Character of Culture', in *Negations: Essays in Critical Theory*, trans. J. J. Shapiro, London: Allen Lane, the Penguin Press, 1968.

5. George Steiner, *The Death of Tragedy*, London: Faber, 1963, pp. 9–10.

6. A. C. Bradley, *Shakespearean Tragedy*, (second edition) London: Macmillan, 1905.

7. Reinhold Niebuhr, *Beyond Tragedy: Essays on the Christian Interpretation of History*, London: Nisbet, 1938; historically, the part played by religion in the Renaissance was quite different from anything Bradley, Niebuhr or Steiner imagine; see Alan Sinfield, *Literature in Protestant England, 1560–1660*, London: Croom Helm, 1983.

8. For accounts of these and other developments in English Studies see Terry Eagleton, *Literary Theory: An Introduction*, Oxford: Blackwell, 1983, and Raman Selden, *A Reader's Guide to Contemporary Literary Theory*, Brighton: Harvester, 1985. More specific in their concerns but equally accessible are Terence Hawkes, *Structuralism and Semiotics*, London: Methuen, 1977, and Catherine Belsey, *Critical Practice*, London: Methuen, 1980.

9. Christopher Hill, 'The Pre-Revolutionary Decades', in *Collected Essays: Vol 1: Writing and Revolution in Seventeenth-Century England*, Brighton: Harvester, 1985, p. 24; *see also* Hill's 'Literature and the English Revolution', in *The Seventeenth Century Journal*, Vol. 1, No. 1, 1986, pp. 15–30, and Walter Cohen's recent and important study, *Drama of a Nation: Public Theatre in Renaissance England and Spain*, Ithaca and London: Cornell University Press, 1985. On literature and politics more generally, as well as the specific issue of literature and the civil war, see Martin Butler, *Theatre and Crisis: 1632–42*, Cambridge University Press, 1984; David Norbrook, *Poetry and Politics in the English Renaissance*, London: Routledge, 1984; Garry Waller, *English Poetry of the Sixteenth Century*, London: Longman, 1986.

10. Lawrence Stone, *The Causes of the English Revolution, 1529–1642*, London: Routledge, 1972, p. 48. *See also* J. P. Sommerville, *Politics and Ideology in England 1603–1640*, London and New York: Longman, 1986.

11. Franco Moretti, *Signs Taken for Wonders: Essays in the Sociology of Literary Forms*, London: NLB and Verso, 1983, trans. Susan Fischer and others, pp. 27–41, 68.

12. Introductions to, as well as examples of, recent work can be found in *Alternative Shakespeares* ed. John Drakakis, London and New York: Methuen, 1985, and *Political Shakespeare: New Essays in Cultural Materialism*, ed. J. Dollimore and A. Sinfield, Manchester University Press and Cornell University Press: 1985. *See also* Malcolm Evans, *Signifying Nothing: Truth's True Contents in Shakespeare's Text*, Brighton: Harvester, 1986. For related work *see also* Simon Shepherd, *Marlowe and the Politics of Elizabethan Theatre*, Brighton: Harvester, 1986.

13. NB: most of the following works have a much wider scope than the subject headings they are included under here, although these subjects do constitute major foci; several books indicate how the three subjects themselves relate inextricably.

   (i) on class see Lucy De Bruyn, *Mob Rule and Riots: The Present Mirrored in the Past*, London and New York: Regency Press, 1981; Margot Heinemann, *Puritanism and Theatre: Thomas Middleton and Opposition Drama Under the Early Stuarts*, Cambridge: Cambridge University Press, 1980; Walter Cohen, *Drama of a Nation*, (see note 9).

   (ii) on sexuality and gender see Coppelia Kahn, *Man's Estate: Masculine Identity in Shakespeare*, University of California Press, 1981; Lisa Jardine, *Still Harping on Daughters: Women and Drama in the Age of Shakespeare*, Brighton: Harvester, 1983; Simon Shepherd, *Amazons and Warrior Women: Varieties of Feminism in Seventeenth Century Drama*, Brighton: Harvester, 1981; Linda Woodbridge, *Women and the English Renaissance: Literature and the Nature of Womankind 1540–1620*, Brighton: Harvester, 1984; Leonard Tennenhouse, *Power on Display: The Politics of Shakespeare's Genres*, London and New York: Methuen, 1986, especially Ch. 3 'Jacobean Tragedy and the Politics of Misogyny'; Catherine Belsey, *The Subject of Tragedy: Identity and Difference in Renaissance Drama*, London and New York: Methuen, 1985; Kathleen McLuskie 'The Patriarchal Bard: Feminist Criticism and Shakespeare: *King Lear* and *Measure for Measure*' and Jonathan Dollimore 'Transgression and Surveillance in *Measure for Measure*' both in *Political Shakespeare*, (see note 12); Peter Erickson, *Patriarchal Structures in Shakespeare's Drama*, Berkeley and London: University of California Press, 1985. For an excellent overview of recent feminist criticism of Shakespeare see Ann Thompson, 'The Warrant of Womenhood: Shakespeare and Feminist Criticism' in *The Shakespeare Myth* ed. Graham Holderness, Manchester University Press, forthcoming.

   (iii) on imperialism and colonialism see Stephen Greenblatt, *Renaissance Self-Fashioning: From More to Shakespeare*, Chicago University Press, 1980; Stephen Greenblatt, 'Invisible Bullets: Renaissance Authority and its Subversion' and Paul Brown, 'This Thing of Darkness I Acknowledge Mine: *The Tempest* and the Discourse of Colonialism' both in *Political Shakespeare* (see note 12); Peter Hulme, *Colonial Encounters: Europe and the Native Caribbean: 1492–1797*, London and New York: Methuen, 1986.

14. See for example Sheila Rowbotham, *Women's Consciousness, Man's World*, Harmondsworth: Penguin, 1973, especially pp. 28–9 and 111; Michèlle Barrett, *Women's Oppression Today*, London: NLB and Verso, 1980; Michèlle Barrett and Mary McIntosh, *The Anti-Social Family*, London: NLB and Verso, 1982.

15. On the importance of this for feminist literary theory see Toril Moi, *Sexual/ Textual Politics*, London and New York: Methuen, 1985; for discussions of subjectivity and subjection in the Renaissance, see Jonathan Dollimore, *Radical Tragedy*, esp. parts 3 and 4 (see note 1) and Francis Barker, *The Tremulous Private Body: Essays on Subjection*, London and New York: Methuen, 1984.

16. *Selected Writings in Sociology and Social Philosophy*, ed. T. B. Bottomore and Maximilien Rubel, Harmondsworth: Penguin, 1963, p. 83.

17. Martin Orkin, 'Cruelty, *King Lear* and the South African Land Act, 1913', forthcoming in *Shakespeare Survey*. This is part of his forthcoming *Shakespeare Against Apartheid*. Orkin is currently engaged on a related project, *Drama and the South African State*, to be published by Manchester University Press.

18. See especially Graham Holderness, *Shakespeare's History*, Dublin and New York: Gill and Macmillan, 1985; Graham Holderness (ed.), *The Shakespeare Myth*, Manchester University Press, forthcoming; *Political Shakespeare* eds. J. Dollimore and A. Sinfield, (see note 12) esp. part 2, 'Reproductions, Interventions'; Terence Hawkes, *That Shakespeherian Rag: Essays on a Critical Process*, London: Methuen, 1986. On criticism up to the early 1970s see J. W. Lever's important review essay, 'Shakespeare and the Ideas of his Time' in *Shakespeare Survey*, 29 (1976) 79–91.

Jonathan Dollimore
Brighton, November 1986

Preface

This short book consists of a series of lectures given when I was visiting professor at Simon Fraser University, British Columbia, between January and March 1970. It was a pleasure and a stimulus to teach in that magnificent setting. I am very grateful to the university for the opportunity, and glad to express my thanks to many colleagues and students of the Department of English, and especially its chairman Gerald Newman, for their unfailing hospitality.

In *The Tragedy of State* I have considered Jacobean tragedy as a product of the intellectual ferment and spiritual upheaval which preceded the first great European revolution. This is an approach which goes against the stream of much prevailing opinion. For a number of years critical scholarship has been largely concerned to stress features of dramatic form and moral outlook which imply an unbroken continuity with medieval tradition. One dramatist after another whose views were once thought to be challenging has been reclassified as a pillar of orthodoxy, affirming concepts of 'order and degree' which opposed any major political or social change. Yet the early seventeenth century in England was a time of radical transformation in attitudes. Then as never before man's inborn freedom, his natural state of equality, his right to rebel against tyrants, were canvassed as vital issues. Of all art forms the theatre was the most public and the most responsive to the spirit of the age. I cannot endorse a view of Jacobean drama which would turn it, like Miss Havisham's house, into a place of drawn curtains and stopped clocks, where tragedy sat for ever re-enacting man's primeval fall.

Only forty years after the stage revolts of *Hamlet* and the revenge plays, Charles I and his court were driven from London. The sons of apprentices who hissed Webster's corrupt Dukes and Cardinals on the stage defeated the cavalier armies in the field. Bussy's affirmations of 'man in his native noblesse' became the guiding principles of the Levellers. But if Jacobean tragedy was a sounding-board for the ideas of a new age of protest, these ideas themselves sprang from a libertarian tradition which deserves to be better known. Too little is remembered, even by modern activists, of the long, bitter struggle against despotism fought out in the Italian cities through the fifteenth and sixteenth centuries. It was a cause which drew in dissidents of every class, spearheaded by students, and resting its hopes of success upon the common people. To dismiss the Renaissance watchword *Viva la liberta!* as an outdated 'bourgeois' slogan is to ignore the expression of a perennial, ultimately irrepressible, human demand.

'State' for the Jacobean dramatists was not the embodiment of a sacrosanct, God-ordained authority. Nor was it merely the instrument of this or that ruling class. Though entrenched in a system of privilege and oppression, it was recognized as an autonomous, self-perpetuating entity, with its own breed of agents and informers. In the petty tyrannies imposed on Renaissance Italy the dramatists found the prototype of the great central monarchies of England and France. Further back still, in the destruction of the Roman Republic by the Caesars, they saw the counterpart in ancient history of the main threat to their own civilization. The tragedies which this outlook inspired have a special relevance in the present age, when the technological super-state exercises an unprecedented degree of control over the minds and bodies of its subjects.

These lectures as printed are slightly changed from their original form. Occasionally I have clarified a phrase, and a few passages and quotations I had to omit when speaking to a time-limit have been restored. In the notes I have sometimes expanded on points I was trying to make, or suggested a wider range of critical opinions. The lectures discuss only a few outstanding plays, and were intended for students without a highly detailed knowledge of Jacobean drama. My aim was to be selective, not encyclopedic, and I thought it better to risk being obvious than obscure.

J. W. LEVER

Malta

For as those Kings that conquer neighbour Nations,
First by the sword make Chaos of creations;
Then, Spider-like, a curious netting spinne,
Invisible, to catch Inferiors in:
So when the Art of powerfull Tyrannie
Hath undermin'd mans native libertie;
Then, like Lords absolute of words, and deeds,
They soone change weeds to herbs, and herbs to weeds. . . .
Disease thus growne, the Crisis, and the Doome,
Shew *Princes must be ours, or we their Tombe.*

Fulke Greville, *Mustapha,* Chorus I
c. 1598

The King, Parliament, great men in the City and Army, have made you but the stairs by which they have mounted to Honor, Wealth and Power. The only Quarrel that hath been, and at present is, is but this, namely, whose slaves the people shall be: All the power that any hath, was but a trust conveyed from you to them, to be employed by them for your good; they have mis-imployed their power, and instead of preserving you, have destroyed you: all Power and Authority is perverted from the King to the Constable, and it is no other but the policy of States-men to keep you divided by creating jealousies and fears among you, to the end that their Tyranny and Injustice may pass un-discovered and unpunished; but the peoples safety is the supream Law; and if a people must not be left without a means to preserve it self against the King, by the same rule they may preserve them-selves against the Parliament and Army too; if they pervert the end for which they received their power, to wit the Nations safety; therefore speedily unite your selves together, and as one man stand up for the defence of your Freedom. . . .

The Bloody Project. Printed in this Yeare
of dissembling, 1648

For

RAY ROBINSON

1911-1943

I

Tragedy and State

The first question a teacher of literature faces today is summed up in the needling word 'relevance'. What is the relevance of his subject, his period, his theme? If he doesn't ask himself, his students will certainly ask him, in no deferential tone. The question is not of course new: replies to it have been formulated since the time of Plato. One convenient reply is that what is interesting must be relevant; if not to our practical needs, then to our mental growth. The proper study of mankind is man; literature is the stuff of human experience; hence its interest, and hence its relevance. All the same, priorities must be reckoned with. In the present-day world, alienated in poverty and affluence, dehumanized by state bureaucracies and military machines, the most urgent study of mankind would seem to be not the eternal human condition, but the prospect of survival in the face of impersonal power drives. What priority can be staked out for the literature of another age – or, to be quite specific, for Jacobean tragedy? While turning this over in my mind, I happened to read an article by *The Times* drama critic describing some current theatre productions in Prague.[1] The writer began by stating his initial sense of embarrassment at visiting Czechoslovakia at this point in her history for no better reason than to report on plays. Very soon, though, he became aware that this was an insular reaction, due mainly to the assumption of most English-speaking people that the theatre is a minor luxury to be forgotten in times of stress. In fact, he found audiences more responsive, even more explosive in their response, than he had ever known before. Drama was clearly felt to be inseparable from life, life from politics, and politics from a sense of the past. He reported an interview with Ottomar Krejca, the director of Prague's 'Theatre Behind The Gate', who described the theatre as 'a political arena that has the strongest effect when it fulfils its purely artistic intentions to the utmost . . . It moves away from everyday life in order to embrace it.'

A striking example of this function of the theatre may be seen in the much-acclaimed Prague production of de Musset's *Lorenzaccio*, a drama of the eighteen-thirties, set in the Florence of the fifteen-thirties. The time is soon after the defeat of the last Florentine republic, which had held out for three years of siege against the professional armies of Austria and Spain. When the play opens, the city has been brought under the rule of a Medici tyrant who serves as the puppet of the occupying powers. Imperial troops keep guard, while disaffected students roam the streets. Political arrests and banishments are the order of the day. Lorenzino, the young hero, is a secret revolutionary who has pledged himself to free Florence by killing its ruler. He wins his way into Duke Alessandro's confidence by acting as his spy and procurer, knowing well that his inner self is being corrupted in the process. At last his opportunity comes. The Duke is lured to a secret rendezvous where he hopes to find a new mistress, and is assassinated in private. But having gained his objective at a terrible price to his soul, Lorenzino finds that nothing positive has been achieved. The people fail to revolt, and a student uprising is easily put down. A new puppet ruler is appointed, as useful to his masters as the one who was slain. The lasting validity of the play is finely expressed in the recent production, where the murdered Duke Alessandro is wrapped in a red robe, from which the same actor steps out in the coronation scene to act the new Duke Cosimo, with Lorenzo's double crouching at his side, ready, as the reviewer puts it, 'for another fruitless round in the endless cycle of oppression and revolt'.

It is easy to understand why this play, set in sixteenth-century Italy by a French writer living in the revolutionary currents of the eighteen-thirties, should have an electrifying effect upon Czech audiences in the winter of 1969–70. However, *Lorenzaccio* is only one example of an approach to drama which views immediate issues as part of a vast continuum and evokes history as an extension of the individual memory. De Musset's play bears a generic resemblance to many Jacobean tragedies, with their court settings, their pervasive atmosphere of idealism and corruption, their ambivalent finales. On the Jacobean stage contemporary issues constantly lurk below the surface of historical or fictitious settings. The events of the play may be taken, as in Chapman's *Bussy* tragedies, from recent political happenings in France; they may, as in Jonson's *Sejanus* or Chapman's *Caesar and Pompey*, be dramatizations of Roman history; or they may present, as in plays of Marston, Tourneur and Webster, incidents inspired by the court intrigues of Renaissance Italian despotisms. But for audiences of the time, the relevance was sufficiently clear. Chapman explicitly drew attention to the parallels between his protagonist Byron and the Earl of Essex,

[2]

executed for treason in 1601. Less direct, but unmistakable in their
tenor, are the recurrent allusions to royal favourites, scheming politicians, sycophants, and the network of informers and secret agents
through which the contemporary state controlled the lives of its
nationals. As Jonson's character Silius observes in *Sejanus*,

> These can lie,
> Flatter and swear, forswear, deprave, inform,
> Smile, and betray; make guilty men; then beg
> The forfeit lives, to get the livings; cut
> Men's throats with whisperings . . .   (I.27–31)

Jonson knew well what he was talking about. He was cited before the
Privy Council in connection with this same play. Already in 1597 he
had been imprisoned for his share in the comedy *The Isle of Dogs*,
described as containing 'very seditious and slanderous matter'; care
was taken that no trace of this play should survive. In 1598 he was in
prison again, where, as he later told Drummond, he was set upon by
'two damned villains to catch advantage of him' – in other words, to
trap him into some statement of opinions that could be used for a charge
of treason. In 1606 Marston was driven to hide away from London for
approximately two years because of his share in the play *Eastward Ho*.
Chapman's two-part play *Byron* led, as a result of protests by the
French ambassador, to the arrest of three of the actors. Chapman
himself managed to escape, but scenes from *The Tragedy of Byron* were
cut out and never appeared in print, while most of Act IV in *Byron's
Conspiracy* has similarly vanished. Even closet dramas not intended for
public performance, or publication, might endanger the author. Fulke
Greville mentions that, following the advice of friends, he destroyed
his *Antony and Cleopatra*, written during the Queen's reign, rather than
run the risk of parallels being found in it to the relationship of Elizabeth
and Essex. It seems to me a fair surmise that Shakespeare for similar
reasons put off the writing, or at least the performance, of his own
Antony and Cleopatra – the historical sequel to *Julius Caesar* – until some
five years after Queen Elizabeth's death.

That the theatre should be intensely concerned with politics was
inevitable in a time of acute tension. Through the fifteen-nineties the
tracking down of Catholic recusants and the suppression of Puritan
groups imposed a strait-jacket of religious orthodoxy. Then in the last
years of Elizabeth's reign and the first years of James I a series of shocks
assailed the body politic. The rebellion of Essex and his followers,

including Southampton, the patron of Shakespeare and Chapman, was followed in 1603 by the tangle of conspiracies known as the Main Plot and By-Plot, in which Cobham and Raleigh with many other noblemen were implicated. In 1605 came the Gunpowder Plot which nearly succeeded in blowing up King and Parliament together. Two years later again, in 1607, peasant disorders and riots against enclosures of the common land swept the Midland counties, to be put down by ruthless repression. Catholics and Puritans, noblemen and peasants, intellectuals with heterodox opinions, had their various, ultimately related grounds for discontent. Over against them stood a governmental system supported by its state church, its lawyers and secret agents, which farmed out monopolies to favoured courtiers and encouraged the nobility to ruin themselves and their estates by conspicuous spending.[2] In the words of Tourneur's Vindice,

> I have seen patrimonies washed a-pieces,
> Fruitfields turned into bastards,
> And in a world of acres
> Not so much dust due to the heir 'twas left to
> As would well gravel a petition.
>
> (*The Revenger's Tragedy*, I.iii.50–4)

Beyond these immediate issues, the serious playwrights of the age were aware of a wider transformation of society taking place throughout Europe and undermining all traditional human relationships. It consisted in the growth and concentration of state power, the destruction of the Italian city republics, the conversion of English, French and Spanish noblemen into court parasites, the absorption of petty despotisms by great monarchies, and the concomitant suppression of a wide range of individual freedoms. The effect upon the victims was to promote a re-thinking of ancient assumptions. What had once been regarded as the privileges of noblemen or burghers or free peasants came to be seen in universal terms as the immemorial rights of what Chapman called 'man in his native noblesse'. In opposition to these stood a concept of absolutism which required that all loyalties, all personal obligations and human bonds be sacrificed to the interests of state. 'The commonwealth', wrote Montaigne, 'requireth some to betray, some to lie, and some to massacre.'[3] In *Sophonisba* Marston paraphrased these words and added the comment:

> I am bound to lose
> My life but not my honour for my country;
> Our vow, our faith, our oath, why they're ourselves ...   (II.i)

[4]

Elsewhere in the same play a character remarks sardonically, 'Thou know'st, a statist must not be a man.' (II.ii). The motivations of power are seen without illusions by Webster's Bosola:

> Some would think the souls of princes were brought forth by some more weighty cause than those of meaner persons – they are deceived, there's the same hand to them: the like passions sway them, the same reason that makes a vicar go to law for a tithe-pig and undo his neighbours, makes them spoil a whole province, and batter down goodly cities with the cannon.
>
> (*Duchess of Malfi*, II.i.101–7)

Driven to these conclusions by the inescapable facts of their time, many thinking men would be prepared to echo Byron's cry:

> The world is quite inverted, Virtue overthrown
> At Vice's feet . . .
> The rude and terrible age is turned again . . .
>
> (*Byron's Tragedy*, I.ii.14–15,17)

All the less would they be inclined to give credence to that hotch-potch of antiquated science, fancy, and folklore dignified by some modern scholars as the Elizabethan World Order. This medieval theory of static hierarchies, each dominated by a supposedly perfect specimen from the stars down to the plants and minerals, had long since declined from a philosophy to a political mystique.

> We see the sun . . . as a monarch among the planets . . . the moon as an empress . . . the fire bearing the sovereignty over the other elements . . . Among the beasts, the lion. Among birds, the eagle . . . There is no power but of God, and the powers that be are ordained of God . . . It is absolutely unlawful for subjects to rise against their prince, be he a tyrant or a heretic.[4]

I have quoted from William Vaughan's stock compilation of received ideas, *The Golden Grove*; many another text would do as well. Corresponding to nothing in the experience or speculative thought of the age, this creed of absolutism served chiefly to bolster up a precarious monarchy which lacked a standing army or an efficient police force.[5] Asserted by Tudor apologists, preached in the homilies officially prescribed for reading in church, reiterated in popular books of universal knowledge for the tired shopkeeper, the so-called 'chain of being' was in an advanced condition of rust by the end of the sixteenth century. It may well be that a silent majority still nodded assent to these platitudes. For the critical, questing minds of Raleigh and Fulke Greville, of Jonson and Marston and Chapman and the mature Shakespeare, such arguments by unproved analogy bore no relation to the facts of nature, of history, or contemporary politics.

What truly exercised these writers was the self-evident phenomenon of state. The word 'state' carried a range of connotations, most of them challenging the traditional view of a divinely sanctioned order. As the term for a commonwealth or polity it was a Renaissance coinage, derived from the idiomatic Italian phrase *lo stato*, which might be rendered in our own idiom as 'the set-up'. The set-up, the system, the establishment, the *status quo*: no aura of divinity, no moral sanction pertained to the actuality of state, by implication subject to change. The same sense of impermanence and flux was to be seen in the state of nature, the vicissitudes of history, the whims of fortune, the pomp and display of kings and their favourites.

> If my dear love were but the child of state,
> It might for fortune's bastard be unfathered,
> As subject to time's love, or to time's hate,
> Weeds among weeds, or flowers with flowers gathered.

Shakespeare's Sonnet 124 reflected a view of life and society subject to continuous alteration and change. The writers of his age were, like him, re-discovering and affirming from their own experience the ideas of classical thinkers: Ovid, who in the last book of the *Metamorphoses* brought in Pythagoras to declare that 'no species is permanently itself, but nature the innovator continually produces one shape from another';[6] Polybius, who, anticipating Spengler by two milleniums, traced a pattern of the rise and fall of empires. Accordingly, Sir William Alexander's poem greeting the accession of James I, *A Paraenesis to the Prince*, expressed a bare tithe of the unquestioning loyalty the occasion might call for. It outlined a theory of kingship arising from the people's choice and dependent for its survival upon the people's consent. Man was originally born free, a dweller in woods and caves who recognized no master. With the building of cities came the establishment of laws and the choice of leaders. Later still, whether through fear of ambitious individuals, or for security in war, or through the advent of some much admired personality, thrones were set up, and the keys of life and death entrusted to one man. Kingdoms first started in small provinces and towns; subsequently, great monarchies swallowed up the small; in the end, the greatest destroyed themselves through overweening ambition.[7] Kings should therefore take heed, avoid the outward signs of glory and cultivate a sense of responsibility.

This is a griefe that all the world bemones,
Whilst those lacke iudgement that are borne to iudge,
And like to painted tombes, or guilded stones,
Are for th'afflicted people no refuge.
Kings are their kingdomes hearts, which tainted once,
The bodies straight must die, in which they lodge:
    And those, by whose example many fall,
    Are guiltie of the murder of them all. (st.19)

Alexander welcomed the accession of King James as a safeguard against the danger of foreign rule; but he stressed the need for even lawful rulers to maintain their virtue and consult their people:

O neuer throne established was so sure,
Whose fall a vitious Prince might not procure. (st.39)

However, Alexander's conclusions were mild as compared with the tremendous implications of Fulke Greville's dramatic poems *Mustapha* and *Alaham*, which were not printed until 1632, four years after Greville's death. Writing of these in his *Life of Sidney* he set forth a new aim for tragedy: 'my purpose in them was not (with the Ancient) to exemplify the disastrous miseries of mans life . . . nor yet (with the Moderne) to point out Gods revenging aspect upon every particular sin . . . but rather to trace out the high waies of ambitious Governours, and to shew in the practice, that the more audacity, advantage, and good successe such Soveraignties have, the more they hasten to their own desolation and ruine' (p. 221). As Greville's editor points out, by the tragedy of the ancients Seneca was meant, and by modern tragedy in all probability such works as *Dr. Faustus, The Jew of Malta, Richard III*, even *Macbeth*.[8] Instead, Greville offered a type of drama modelled on the Senecan form but devoted to a searching, impassioned analysis of the workings of state. Following Renaissance practice, he chose his subjects not from mythology but from history, whose contemporary relevance could easily be noted. Objectivity was gained by the Turkish settings, events taking place at the court of the Sultan, an absolute despot supported by the authoritarian creed of Islam. But Greville left no room for doubt that his concepts of state and the state church applied to the West as well as the East. As his Mahometan priests declare:

The Christian bondage is much more refined,
Though not in real things, in real names;
Laws, doctrine, discipline, being all assigned
To hold upright that witty man-built frame;

Where every limb, though in themselves distinct,
Yet finely are unto the sceptre linked.

An art by which man seems, but is not free;
Crowns keeping all their specious guiding reins,
Fast in the hand of strong authority;
So to relax, or wind up passion's chains,
  As before humble people know their grief,
  Their states are used to look for no relief.

(*Mustapha*, Chorus II, 109–20)

In the five headlong choruses of *Mustapha*, religion and law are seen as universal instruments of rule and means to secure the hold of despotism upon the people. The rise of great states and the growth of empires are characterized as a fatal disease of society. Ultimately it is the people themselves who must decide their future, for it is only with their acquiescence that absolutism prevails:

Whence I conclude: mankind is both the form,
And matter, wherewith tyrannies transform:
For power can neither see, work, or devise,
Without the people's hands, hearts, wit and eyes:
So that were man not by himself oppressed,
Kings would not, tyrants could not make him beast.

(Chorus II, 205–10)

Greville and Alexander, like Daniel and other writers of the Countess of Pembroke's circle, did not intend their plays for public performance. While making them a vehicle for the ideas of the age, they modelled their form on the strict classical precedents they found in Seneca. The professional playwrights, on the other hand, had to accommodate their outlook to the complexities and fluidity of the living theatre. Yet for them too, Seneca was a potent, omnipresent influence. No amount of research into the survival of medieval stage traditions can wipe out this vast presence, which shaped the imagination of Renaissance Europe.[9] Nor should the spiritual reach of early Greek tragedy blind us to the fact that dramatists in the age of despotism found their true affinity in this Roman writer at the court of Nero. Seneca was the poet of the extreme situation; the projector of the terrible moment when the hammer-blows of tyrannical force bring man to the edge of endurance. Aeschylus and Sophocles had measured human suffering in the balance of divine justice: Seneca rejected any evidence of justice in the action of the gods, who were indeed hardly more than names for

[8]

the destructive urges in the cosmos and in man himself. Against these blind, malignant forces he opposed the power of rationality, the Stoic affirmation of a kingdom of the mind, unshaken by tyranny, unmoved by horrors:

> Not riches makes a king, or high renown ...
> A king is he that fear hath laid aside,
> And all affects that in the breast are bred ...
> It is the mind that only makes a king.
>
> (*Thyestes*, Chorus II)[10]

Hoc regnum sibi quisque dat: this kingdom each man bestows upon himself. Seneca's maxim strikes the keynote of Jacobean tragedy with its contrast between the state of outward seeming and the inner monarchy of man. 'I never was a prince till now', declares Marston's Andrugio as a fugitive in danger of death. 'Every inch a king', affirms Shakespeare's Lear at the height of his madness. Webster's tragic duchess preserves her integrity through mental torture with the words 'I am Duchess of Malfi still.'

Writing in a different civilization for a different theatre, the Jacobean playwrights broke the classical mould of drama to offer a much wider range of characters and settings. Action was centred in the court life of the modern state, amid the swirl of political and sexual intrigue. Immediate precedents lay to hand in the spectacular melodramas of Marlowe and the intricate theatrical effects of Kyd. Clowning and comic relief, masques and disguises all made their contribution. Intermingled with them were Senecan devices creating what seem to us odd discrepancies. Ghosts and supernatural omens incongruously guide the actions of Italian dukes or French noblemen. But these are only the more superficial features. Far more important is the persistence of the Senecan view of life and its compelling vision of tragedy. The Senecan tyrant had not changed his character down the ages from the Roman empire to the Renaissance, though he and his agents had added to their ferocity a cold cynicism we may if we like call Machiavellian, remembering always that Machiavelli, at heart a republican patriot, only formulated the practice of the modern ruler.[11] As for the Senecan attitudes of resistance, defiance, or unflinching endurance of tyranny—whether it be the tyranny of earthly rulers, or of fortune and the stars, – these too had not essentially changed. In the Rome of the Caesars an educated élite turned away from the official religion to seek a personal philosophy, and found their needs answered in the Stoic way of life. So in the late Renaissance age of despots thinking men abandoned the traditional world outlook with its fixed hierarchies and drew moral stamina from a revived Stoicism. This did not necessarily mean a total rejection of religious faith. Rather like modern existentialism, Stoic doctrines could be reconciled on a metaphysical plane with Christianity. But like existentialism, which exercised its maximum influence in the time of Nazi oppression, its appeal was less as an abstract philosophy than as a guide to conduct. Epictetus and Seneca were not systematic thinkers, but they offered a dignified response to the paradoxes and absurdities of the human condition; they supplied a stance for the alienated individual in a society and a cosmos drained of meaning. Renaissance Stoicism was not so much an academic theory as a practical discipline for men involved in the world of action, caught, whether they wished it or not, in the meshes of 'state'.

Most of the plays I shall be considering present us with modes of tragedy unrelated to Aristotle's familiar definitions. They are not primarily treatments of characters with a so-called 'fatal flaw', whose downfall is brought about by the decree of just if inscrutable powers. The heroes may have their faults of deficiency or excess; but the fundamental flaw is not in them but in the world they inhabit: in the political state, the social order it upholds, and likewise, by projection, in the cosmic state of shifting arbitary phenomena called 'Fortune'.[12] For the most part, indeed, we are not greatly concerned with the characters as individuals. Generally their emotional relationships and psychological make-up are sketched in broad outlines which hardly call for a close-range scrutiny. What really matters is the quality of their response to intolerable situations. This is a drama of adversity and stance, not of character and destiny. The heroes vary a good deal in stature and in their respective claims on our admiration. Their attitudes range over the whole gamut from total commitment to the destruction of evil, even at the cost of destroying in the process their own integrity, to an opting out of the conflict by self-chosen death, or retreat into an impregnable kingdom of the mind. There are varying degrees of defiance and endurance: philosophical consistency is less important than the establishment of the individual stance. As for the powers that be, whether on earth or above it, at court or in the stars, the force they exercise is unrelated to what men understand by reason or justice. The rational man who remains master of himself is by the same token the ultimate master of his fate. In the words of Chapman's Byron:

I am a nobler substance than the stars,
And shall the baser overrule the better ?
Or are they better, since they are the bigger ?
I have a will, and faculties of choice,
To do, or not to do; and reason why
I do, or not do this; the stars have none ...
(*Byron's Conspiracy*, III.iii.109–14)

I have suggested a community of outlook in Jacobean tragedy; but this does not of course imply a common dramatic method. It is only to be expected that in the theatre of the early seventeenth century, with its diversity of traditions and techniques, the tragedy of state should be enacted in diverse forms, operating through a variety of theatrical effects. Perhaps the most clearly defined form, the one we think of first when we speak of Jacobean tragedy, is the revenge play, or, as it is sometimes called, the tragedy of blood. Certainly blood is much in evidence in this class of plays, both on the stage and in the minds of the characters. It is liberally prescribed in the memorable stage directions at the beginning of Marston's *Antonio's Revenge*: '*Enter* Piero, *unbrac't, his armes bare, smear'd in blood, a poniard in one hand bloodie and a torch in the other,* Strotzo *following him with a corde*'.

And blood persists down to the hero's last entry in Ford's *'Tis Pity She's a Whore*, probably to be taken as the last play of this kind:

Enter Giovanni *with a heart upon his dagger.*
GIOVANNI: Here, here, Soranzo; trimm'd in reeking blood
That triumphs over death; proud in the spoil
Of love and vengeance ! Fate or all the powers
That guide the motions of immortal souls
Could not prevent me.   (V.vi.9–13)

While Giovanni's defiance of fate strikes a Senecan note, the theatrical effect of his entry with a bleeding heart on his dagger does not derive from classical drama, where horrors are almost always intimated only by report. It belongs rather to the Elizabethan tradition which, like the modern 'theatre of cruelty', prided itself on its capacity to shock. Frequently the Jacobean revenge play also met the psychological need for compensatory laughter. Clowning, parody, black farce, were concomitant effects, a necessary counterpoint to horror which, if we only think of these plays as printed texts, may appear crude and bathetic. Again, in the treatment of revenge which underlies the action, we are faced with the Elizabethan tradition of complex intrigue and counter-intrigue, disguises and masques, which make a notable contrast to the simple plot-machinery of such classical revenge plays as *Orestes* or *Medea*. The question may be asked whether the word 'tragedy' is not a mere literary label we are attaching to a mode of 'pure' theatre which makes its appeal at the subliminal level and does not speak to the rational mind. Is the Jacobean revenge play, with its affinities to the 'theatre of cruelty', an anticipation of the doctrines of Artaud, who wished to offer the spectator what he called 'the truthful precipitates of dreams, in which his taste for crime, his erotic obsessions, his savagery . . . even his cannibalism'[13] would be met ? At the opposite extreme of interpretation, there is the didactic concept, which sees this class of play as the treatment of an important issue for the seventeenth-century moralist: whether, and to what extent, revenge may be justified. Fredson Bowers, in his pioneer study *Elizabethan Revenge Tragedy* (1940), supplies a great deal of information, based on sermons, tracts, and other contemporary writings, concerning Elizabethan attitudes to revenge. The conclusion reached, which might have been guessed from the start, is that the normal respectable, God-fearing citizen in the time of Elizabeth or King James thought revenge was a very bad and impious course of action. Accordingly it is to be inferred that audiences regarded revenge plays as cautionary fables, and watched the unfolding of the intrigues with a mounting sense of disapproval and a growing conviction of the soundness of their own orthodox opinions.

In my view neither of these interpretations hits the mark. I do not see the Jacobean revenge play as so-called 'pure theatre' where the spectators are meant to peel off their rational minds, their political and social preoccupations, for a vicarious sauna-bath in the collective unconscious. Nor, at the other extreme, would I regard these plays as exemplary warnings on the evils of taking the law into one's own hands. What Bowers fails to allow for is that in Jacobean tragedy it is not primarily the conduct of the individual, but of the society which assails him, that stands condemned. Certainly the taking of private revenge was an evil of the age, and the extent to which the code of honour should be respected was a very live issue. But the typical situation of the revenge play is unrelated to the operation of the feud or the possibilities of recourse to law. The hero is faced with iniquity on high, with crimes committed by a tyranny immune to criticism or protest. His father may have been murdered, his mistress dishonoured, his friend ruined by the despot or his minions. Through personal wrongs the play dramatizes the general corruption of state, and confronts the hero with the imperative necessity to act, even at the price of his own moral contamination. The treatment of these issues may be sensationalized, but the issues themselves involve the dramatist's preoccupation with objective reality. Concerned, in Greville's words, 'to trace out the high ways of ambitious governours', the Jacobean revenge drama evokes an authentic form of tragic experience.

Different in its operation is what might be called the heroic play, where attention is focused on a great man, presented as superhuman in his courage, his nobility, his faults of impulsiveness or alternatively his virtuous disregard of human baseness. Chapman's Bussy and Clermont are men of this calibre, though deliberately contrasted in temper and response. Here too the Elizabethan stage offered a model in Marlowe's supermen. Like Tamburlaine, who aspired

> To cast up hills against the face of heaven
> And dare the force of angry Jupiter,

Chapman's heroes command attention by their stage presence and their splendid rhetoric. They dominate the plays they are in; their passions or their principles are seemingly paramount. Again the charge of sensationalism arises. It may be asked whether such drama is more than a spectacular exhibition of personality. Again, too, the opposite interpretation has been put forward, urging us to view Chapman's tragedies in terms of the received ideas of the age, as exemplary treatments of egotism and passion. Here too it is assumed that the individual and not the world he lives in is on trial. Chapman's plays are given a well-defined political setting, that of the almost contemporary French court, where, despite the apparently superhuman dimensions of the heroes, they are overthrown by the quiet but deadly machinations of policy. Hercules, Seneca's archetypal hero, was destroyed through the jealousy of the gods, unwilling to tolerate such greatness in man. Marlowe's Tamburlaine died because finally he was not immune to mortality. But Bussy and Clermont, trapped by politicians and informers, are the victims of state. It is an orderly, well-organized state, unlike the Italian despotisms of Marston's and Tourneur's revenge plays. The King is seen playing chess, not brandishing a bloody poniard. In spite of this, perhaps because of this, Chapman's heroes are more assuredly doomed than those of Marston and Tourneur. Fate, as incalculable and malevolent as in Seneca, operates through the court. 'Who are Fate's ministers?' asks Bussy. 'The Guise and Monsieur', he is told.

Another type of Jacobean tragedy takes its themes from Roman

[13]

history. Both Jonson and Chapman at some time in their writing career experimented with this subject. The Elizabethan antecedent was the English history play which dramatized material taken from the six-teenth-century chronicles. The Jacobean treatment of Roman themes differed from this in two outstanding respects. One is that, for all the differences in treatment and approach between writers of such marked individuality, all alike implicitly reject the providential view of history. There is no suggestion of divine blessing or punishment in the rise and fall of rulers, comparable to the attitudes of Holinshed or Hall. Granted that the setting was a pre-Christian society; but this had not prevented sixteenth-century writers from drawing pious inferences. In these Jacobean plays neither Caesar nor Tiberius exercised power in the name of a beneficent providence shaping history for the good of man. On the contrary, power is seen as a completely amoral entity, divorced from all virtue, at once the offspring and the seed of corruption. Secondly, these plays are marked by a thoroughgoing pessimism. No hope seems to survive for a better future in society. Jonson's party of just men in *Sejanus* are helpless and serve only as a chorus giving expression to the author's hatred of the absolute state. Chapman's *Caesar and Pompey* returns to the beginnings of the process which led to the domination of Rome by such creatures as Tiberius and Sejanus. Pompey, immersed in the struggle for power through most of the play, only discovers true human values after the battle of Pharsalia, when he has irrevocably lost in one day the reputation gained over a lifetime. Cato, the play's Stoic hero, takes his life rather than accept the dictator-ship of Caesar. Only in the brief reunion of Pompey and his wife Cornelia on the isle of Lesbos, at the far limit of civilized Europe, is there a spark of affirmation. In their common recognition of the vanity of greatness, human love and constancy seem to transcend the flux of history and fortune. But there is no escape even here from the power-dominated world. Like Cleopatra's dream of an Emperor Antony, Pompey's vision of a human love on which the universe may turn sub-sists only in the imagination.

In Webster's two late-Jacobean tragedies the Italian setting and relationships of the revenge play are recalled. After the work of Chap-man and Jonson, however, there could be no return to the simple juxta-positions of Marston and Tourneur. While the Renaissance state is presented in a wealth of realistic detail, satirized in baroque conceits, castigated in sententious couplets, the old antitheses of tyrant and revenger, vice and virtue are overlaid. In *The White Devil* corruption is seen as a universal phenomenon, the ambience of an entire civilization. As in Jonson's satires, the innocent evoke only a passing pity; the characters who dominate the stage differ as between cunning hypocrites and wrongdoers who are at least frank in their lust and pride. In *The Duchess of Malfi*, however, there is a shift of perspective; a focusing, as in Chapman, upon the individual predicament. Social and cosmic issues are viewed through the eyes of particular characters. Love is seen as the only possible mode of human existence; power recognized as self-destructive. The choice lies not between good and evil, but between reason and madness, ultimately between life and death. In this final analysis, the catastrophic ending of tragedy admits at least some modest hope of a better future, not only in an after-life, but even on earth. The insane criminals of the established order lie dead, as well as their victim and their dupe. But the son of a Duchess who preferred love and motherhood to the sterility of rank and power, and of her husband, an honest commoner, has survived. 'Let us make noble use Of this great ruin', says Delio in the last speech of the play. The silent unnamed boy at the side of his father's friend is the modest token of another, more humanly acceptable order.

NOTES

1. *The Times* (Saturday Review), November 29, 1969: 'The Czech Dream', by Irving Wardle.

2. For a detailed description of extravagance, waste, corruption and vice at the court of James I, see G. P. V. Akrigg, *Jacobean Pageant* (1962), chapters XIV and XVIII. Unprecedented sums of money were squandered on dress, banquets, lavish entertainments and dissipation. Titles and government offices were bought and sold. Through monopolies, tax-farming and enclosures the entire national economy was fleeced by a parasitic court and its hangers-on.

3. Montaigne, *Essays* (translated Florio) III.I (Everyman Edition, vol. 3, p. 8).

4. William Vaughan, *The Golden-groue* (1600), chapter 3.

5. 'We must remember . . . how much more serious a problem civil discord was in the Renaissance than it is now and how much more important was the myth of the God-ordered universe in keeping the state functioning. In a state with no police force and no standing army it is easy to understand why moralists never tired of repeating that the individual's passions were everyone's concern.' Franklin M. Dickey, *Not Wisely But Too Well:*

Shakespeare's Love Tragedies (1957), p. 96. (Dickey clearly underrates the 'problem' of civil discord in our day, and overlooks the analogous conditioning by mass media in modern states well equipped with riot police, para-military forces and a vast range of repressive techniques for curbing 'the individual's passions'.)

6. *'Nec species sua cuique manet, rerumque novatrix Ex aliis alias reparat natura figuras.'* Ovid, *Metamorphoses* XV, 252–3.

7. Robert Ornstein in *The Moral Vision of Jacobean Tragedy* (1962), p. 282, n. 7, has pointed out the prevalence of the idea of natural equality. It was stated in Christian terms in Erasmus, *The Education of a Christian Prince*, and developed as a secular theory by Bodin, tracing the rise, expansion and fall of states and empires through military conquest. See *The Six Bookes of a Commonweale* (translated Knolles, 1606). Alexander's account seems indebted to Bodin.

8. *The Poems and Dramas of Fulke Greville,* ed. Geoffrey Bullough (1939), Vol. II, pp. 1–2.

9. The importance of Seneca in English drama is minimised by Howard Baker, *Induction To Tragedy* (1939, 1965) and G. K. Hunter, 'Seneca and the Elizabethans: A Case-Study in "Influence"', *Shakespeare Survey* 20 (1967), pp. 17–26. The arguments are mainly directed to suggesting alternative origins in the classics or medieval tradition for theatrical conventions or sententious phrases generally attributed to Seneca. But the widespread concurrence of Senecan motifs, images, and direct quotations or paraphrases in Kyd, Shakespeare, Marston, Chapman and others, against a European background of frankly admitted indebtedness, cannot be thus dismissed. More important than particular borrowings is the resemblance in spiritual orientation, outlook on life, and conception of tragic experience. Perhaps the most illuminating brief description of Seneca's influence is to be found in Hardin Craig's 'The Shackling of Accidents: A Study of Elizabethan Tragedy', *Philological Quarterly* XIX (1940), pp. 1–19, reprinted in *Elizabethan Drama: Modern Essays in Criticism,* ed. Ralph J. Kaufmann (1961), pp. 22–40. See also F. P. Wilson, *Elizabethan and Jacobean* (1945), Eugene M. Waith, *The Herculean Hero in Marlowe, Chapman, Shakespeare and Dryden* (1962), and G. K. Hunter's introduction to Marston's *Antonio's Revenge*, Regents Renaissance Drama Series (1965), xii–xv, for considerations of Senecan and Stoic influences on the tragedies of Jonson, Chapman and Marston.

10. Translated by Jasper Heywood, *Newton's Seneca*, Tudor Translations (1927) pp. 66–7.

11. 'In the seat of Lorenzo the Magnificent sat the petty poisoners and tyrants of Medicean degeneracy; and the Machiavelli who had died crying *"Amo la patria mia più dell' anima"* became in men's memory only the devilish

archetype of Iago and Barabbas.' F. L. Lucas, Introduction to *The Works of John Webster* (1927, 1966), Vol. I, p. 37.

12. 'Seneca's consolation for the blows of fate is different from that of Aeschylus. It is philosophic instead of religious. The naturalistic submission of Aeschylus is gone. Instead of a human behaviour controlled and directed within human limits and justified by veneration to the gods, Seneca introduces a stoical remedy against the badness of man's lot . . . man was sure to be beaten, but Seneca proposed to build up something within the heart of man which would enable him to gain a pyrrhic victory over fate. This doctrine is inherent in the stories of Hercules and Prometheus and is closely allied with titanism.' Hardin Craig, 'The Shackling of Accidents', ed. Kaufmann, *loc. cit.*, p. 32. Here Craig in effect bridges the disparity between Seneca's philosophic quietism and the aspirations of his tragic heroes. The responses of philosopher and man of action were alike induced by the alienating factor of tyranny, actual in the world empire of Rome, conceptualized in notions of fate and the gods.

13. Antonin Artaud, *The Theatre and its Double*, First Manifesto; translated by M. C. Richards (1958).

II

Revenge Drama:
Antonio's Revenge, The Revenger's Tragedy

Jacobean revenge tragedy, as is generally known, took its dramatic form from the theatrical experiments of Kyd in the fifteen-eighties. In *The Spanish Tragedy* and most probably in the early *Hamlet* the new playwrights found the main ingredients they needed for the contemporary stage: a wide range of characters, a court setting, a dynamic of complicated intrigue and delayed revenge, with a final spectacular catastrophe. All this the Jacobeans made their own, adding an infusion of satire, intellectual speculation and moral aphorisms. The result was a dramatic treatment of the special shape in which evil revealed itself in their age: the phenomenon of state power and the debasement of human values. The playwrights are not altogether sure whether the evil they present is the work of a particular ruler, or a system of rule, or in the order of nature itself. The ethics of revolt impose moral conflicts, and the problem of a universe where violence and arbitrary suffering are part of the human lot evokes a variety of responses, from total scepticism to a Christianized Stoicism that abandons hope in earthly happiness and looks for comfort in the afterlife.

Revenge drama was not written to a set formula, and there are marked differences of treatment. All the same, we can distinguish a basic pattern which recurs, with modifications, in play after play. First – but not foremost – there is the type of true authority, the virtuous ruler who is seen as a foil to the corrupt court. As an individual he is a memory, or a future prospect, rather than a present factor. Such is Hamlet's father, or Andrugio in *Antonio's Revenge*, alive in the thoughts of others; alternatively, Giovanni the boy heir who assumes authority in the last scene of *The White Devil*, or the old nobleman Antonio who restores order at the end of *The Revenger's Tragedy*, A major role, however, is given to the anti-type, the tyrant or usurper. In character he preserves many of the original traits of the Senecan tyrant. He is the slave of passion, possessed by jealousy and fear, unable to tolerate

[18]

around him any companions but flatterers and fools. At the same time he shows a Renaissance sophistication in his wide-ranging ambitions, his capacity for hypocrisy and intrigue, his overall cynicism. A third role, likewise borrowed from Seneca, is the ghost, a figure of import-ance in the earlier plays where he directly incites to revenge. He may take the shape of the virtuous ruler, but his part requires that he be transformed into a very different being, to some extent a pagan fury, to some extent a projection of the subjective passions of the revenger. In his obsessive demands of blood for blood he is wholly immune to the normal human urges of pity and mercy. Most important of all, there is the play's protagonist, the revenger himself, who stands directly opposed to the tyrant. Shakespeare indeed made Hamlet the most com-plex of his characters; but even in the more typical revenge plays, con-cerned rather with attitude than personality, the revenger is made up of twisted strands. He may bring together the qualities of victim, rebel, satirist, lover, Stoic and counter-villain. In his thought and conduct the rival claims of action and reflection, commitment and opting out, struggle for ascendancy. As the play unfolds groupings are formed which involve the family and friends of both the tyrant and the revenger. The integrity of these secondary figures, their honour and virtue at a personal level, is tested and their attitude to the issue of tyranny takes shape. The isolation of Shakespeare's Hamlet is exceptional; usually two opposed parties are brought into being. Finally, after plot and counterplot, deceit and counter-deception, the revenge is consum-mated. It takes place on a crowded stage; conventionally it is carried out by the revengers in the guise of masked dancers who convert the tyrant's festivities into a scene of carnage. Seeming is juxtaposed to seeming; the decorous formalities of Renaissance masquerade become a savage ritual of vengeance against tyrants.

It is usual to dismiss the Italian setting of the typical revenge play as a never-never-land of the northern imagination. ' "Italy" ', writes G. K. Hunter, 'is little more than convenient shorthand to express a symbolic world where the individual is lost in the mazes of political activity.'[1] Italy does indeed express this; but the choice of country and the political manners depicted have more solid foundations than the fancies of the English playwright. F. L. Lucas wisely remarked, in answer to those who object, like Judge Brack in *Hedda Gabler*, that 'people do not do such things': 'They did . . . read the history of the time.'[2] Taking his advice, one reads. The annals of the Italian age of despots describe tyrannies and atrocities, plots and revolts, which make the inventions of the Jacobeans rather pedestrian. One reads of Gian Maria Visconti, the dictator of Milan, who kept a pack of dogs fed on human flesh and trained them to hunt down and savage his political prisoners. Universally hated for his oppressions and cruelties, he was murdered in 1412 while on his way to receive holy communion. His successor Filippo Maria Visconti imprisoned the ruler of Lodi in a cage at Pavia where he died, like Marlowe's Bajazet, beating his brains out against the bars. At Rimini in 1444 Raimondo Malatesta was stabbed by his two nephews, disguised, like the assassins of Webster's *White Devil*, in the habit of friars. At Bologna in 1445 the entire Bentivogli family, a well-liked dynasty, was murdered at a christening feast to which they had been invited, as a pretended gesture of conciliation, by their rivals the Canedoli, at the instigation of the Duke of Milan. In revenge the citizens hunted down the whole Canedoli clan, sacked and burnt some fifty of their residences, and tore to pieces Battista, its aged head, who was apparently innocent.[3] The stories of Vittoria Accorombona and the Duchess of Amalfi, heroines of Webster's tragedies, continue the tradition into the sixteenth century. These and many more deeds of tyranny and revolt passed into the collective memory of Renaissance Europe, much as the massacres and atrocities of modern rulers have passed into ours. Nevertheless, the writers of revenge tragedy should not be judged by standards of historical realism. Their aim was not to re-create history, but to express contemporary anxieties by transposing them into a period and setting which had become the type and pattern of naked despotism. Had the Italy of the revenge play been pure fantasy, their serious concerns might have been swamped in the sensationalism of their fictions. Actually, the basis of truth underlying a stylized approach added to the play's validity.

I turn from these generalities to two revenge plays of the time: Marston's *Antonio's Revenge*, and *The Revenger's Tragedy*, by an author whom for convenience I shall call Cyril Tourneur. Whether Tourneur did in fact write this play, which was not attributed to him until 1656, or whether we prefer some other candidate for the honour, need not be gone into here. But if the author is a shadow, his play is substantial enough, and has a particular interest in its distinctive approach. The two together make a striking parallel and contrast.

On the whole, Marston has had what might be called a bad press among literary scholars. As Robert Ornstein remarks, 'Critics who have no taste for Marston's virtues have no charity for his vices.'[4] T. S. Eliot in his loftiest manner expressed 'bewilderment that anyone could write plays so bad, and that plays so bad could be preserved and re-printed.' But he also added, rather revealingly, 'they are not plays that one easily forgets.'[5] Eliot did not unbend so far as to tell us what sort of badness he had in mind, whether artistic badness or the badness of an ethical outlook at odds with his own, or whether the latter necessitated the former. There are, it is true, qualities about Marston's earlier plays which jar upon us all. There is a tendency to violent, clotted diction, carried over from the verse satires, where this had been deliberately cultivated in keeping with the rude invective style the Elizabethans thought proper for this kind of poetry. – 'Dog, I will make thee eat thy vomit up Which thou hast belk'd 'gainst blameless Mellida.' – The imagery here and elsewhere shows a visceral or anal preoccupation which Marston shared with Ben Jonson and Pope and Swift, and which, I am inclined to think, had very little to do with psychological make-up but served as a literary device for communicating intense disgust. There is also in this earlier work, probably due to the influence of Seneca, a use of heightened rhetoric to suggest tragic elevation. But, as Eliot had to admit, there is also a memorable quality. For all the hyperbole, one senses a very genuine creative energy, an intense response to experience. Sometimes the energy is channelled into a terse simplicity which Marston had also learnt from Seneca, as in the Stoic dirge of Act IV:

> Death, exile, plaints and woe
> Are but man's lackeys, not his foe.
> No mortal scapes from fortune's war
> Without a wound, at least a scar.
> Many have led these to the grave,
> But all shall follow, none shall save.   (IV. ii.97 ff.)[6]

The same qualities ensured that Marston's plays were carefully and economically designed, blending a classical sense of form with a full deployment of the resources of the Jacobean theatre. In a constant experimentation with different kinds of drama, during which Marston hardly ever repeated or parroted himself, most of the initial awkwardness soon fell away.

Published in 1601 as part two of *Antonio and Mellida*, *Antonio's Revenge* has little in common with the earlier play except for the re-appearance of some of the characters. *Antonio and Mellida* is a romantic comedy broadly resembling *As You Like It*. Duke Andrugio, the philosophical ruler of Genoa, has been overthrown by Piero, Duke of Venice, and driven into hiding. His son Antonio is in love with Piero's daughter Mellida. The lovers escape to a pastoral exile where they meet Andrugio. Romantic love, elements of satire and Stoic moralising are brought together against an Arcadian background, and there is a happy reversal at the end when the tyrannical Duke Piero, impressed by Antonio's courage in presenting himself boldly at his enemy's court, forgives the young man, consents to the match, and offers reconciliation to old Andrugio. All this is on the familiar lines of Elizabethan romance; but one senses that Marston did not find the form altogether congenial. The humour is without true gaiety, the wit rather laboured, and the romantic theme a little forced. There is a more pervasive note of bitterness at villainy and sorrow for its victims than we find in Shakespeare's romantic comedies. Nevertheless the play as it stands carries no hint of a tragic sequel.

Antonio's Revenge opens, as we have seen, with a startling theatrical effect: the entry of Duke Piero, his arms smeared with blood and a bloody dagger in his hand, followed by his brutal henchman Strotzo, a name recalling the Italian verb 'to strangle'. He has just stabbed to death the son of Pandulpho, a wise old councillor at the court, on the false charge that the young man has committed fornication with his daughter Mellida. On the same night, at the banquet of supposed reconciliation, Andrugio had been poisoned, the effects working in such a way as to suggest that he died of an excess of joy at the end of his misfortunes. Having murdered Antonio's father and slandered his sweetheart, besides killing an entirely innocent young man, Piero looks ahead to the completion of his dark design, in which Antonio will be incriminated, Mellida cleared of blame, and Andrugio's widow married to her late husband's murderer. The motivation of all this villainy is twofold. Piero has always been jealous of Andrugio since the time when he was an unsuccessful suitor of Maria, Andrugio's wife. But more important than passion is the urge of policy. By marrying Andrugio's widow, and disinheriting Andrugio's son Antonio, Piero will rule Genoa, and by matching his own daughter Mellida to the son of the Duke of Florence, he will make himself master of three states.

> Antonio pack'd hence, I'll his mother wed,
> Then clear my daughter of supposed lust,
> Wed her to Florence's heir, O excellent!
> Venice, Genoa, Florence at my beck,
> At Piero's nod.   (II.i.13 ff.)

Meanwhile the counter-intrigue develops as an ingenious combination of two revenge themes. The living survivors of Piero's villainy are the old courtier Pandulpho who, like Hieronymo in *The Spanish Tragedy*, has lost his son, and the young heir Antonio who, like Hamlet, has lost his father. For the overthrow of the tyrant it is necessary for the two to join forces. But the ingenuity of plot is not simply mechanical; it is made to subserve a treatment of two kinds of response to calamity. Antonio, romantic, impulsive and immature, reacts to suffering with a wild indulgence of passion, or if we like to call it so, hysteria, which makes him incapable of action. Pandulpho in contrast, schooled in Stoic self-discipline, refuses to bow to grief, but inclines to passive endurance.

> No, my loved youth, he may of valour vaunt
> Whom fortune's loudest thunder cannot daunt.
> Whom fretful galls of chance, stern fortune's siege,
> Makes not his reason shrink, the soul's fair liege;
> Whose well-peised action ever rests upon
> Not giddy humours, but discretion. (I.ii.329–34)

In the interplay of attitudes and the active alliance finally forged between age and youth, Stoic philosopher and romantic lover, lies the thematic development of the play.

Antonio's passion, Pandulpho's sententiousness, the execution of Piero's accomplice after believing to the end that his master would rescue him, the final masque of revengers, are all clearly adapted from Kyd's *Spanish Tragedy*. But the character-relationships and the general run of incidents seem to us like reminiscences of Shakespeare's *Hamlet*. We have Antonio, heir to the dukedom of Genoa, whose father has been poisoned; his mother Maria, about to be married to her husband's murderer; his fiancée Mellida; his friend and confidant Alberto; and the ghost of the dead Andrugio. Again, the ghost's revelation of the crime, the encounter of Antonio, his mother and the ghost in his mother's bedchamber, Antonio's entry reading a book and the following soliloquy, all suggest *Hamlet*. Nevertheless it is highly probable that *Antonio's Revenge* was written by Marston without any knowledge of Shakespeare's play. The dates suggest that it precedes the *Hamlet* we know; what is more, at no point does Marston echo Shakespeare's imagery or speech-rhythms, or try to repeat his speculations and conceits. The truth seems to be that both Marston's play and Shakespeare's were inspired by the lost play *Hamlet* written in the early fifteen-nineties, and that each writer followed his own artistic bent. *Antonio's Revenge* shows none of the subtlety and speculative range of Shakespeare's play, but it has positive virtues of its own. The motivation is clear-cut, and for all the horrors and grotesqueries, the main thread of action never gets lost. The characters too are without Shakespeare's puzzling contradictions. Maria, the counterpart to Queen Gertrude, remains loyal to her husband and does not marry Piero. She allows herself to be wooed by him, but this is carefully distanced from the dramatic action by being intimated only in a formal dumb-show, so that the audience's sympathy is not forfeited. Mellida, who stands in the place of Ophelia, does not collaborate with the tyrant in spying on her lover, and Antonio never doubts her virtue or lectures her on the frailties of woman. Pandulpho scornfully refuses to join Piero in his schemes against Antonio; he is a steadfast philosopher, not, like Polonius, a tedious and somewhat shifty old politician. Antonio therefore is not driven into isolation but finds virtuous allies. The play is not much concerned with his character, or with the intricacies of character in general, but with the presentation of attitudes towards tyranny and the rallying of all forces that oppose it. In the end even the innocent fool Balurdo, who had been imprisoned for blurting out a protest against Piero, joins the masquers and takes part in the revenge.

Balurdo's presence, as well as that of Nutrice, Maria's attendant who resembles the nurse in *Romeo and Juliet*, raises the question of how we are to take Marston's comic effects. It has been argued that *Antonio's Revenge* has been completely misinterpreted by modern readers; that the play was not intended as a tragedy but as a burlesque. We are asked to remember that Marston's play was first performed by child actors, whose rendering of high-flown tragic parts would seem absurd; that Marston counted on this to entertain a sophisticated audience; and that the comic characters and episodes reinforced the inherent parody.[7] This, I am quite sure, is itself a misconception. If *Antonio's Revenge* were meant as a parody we should expect at least some hint of this in its prologue. But in fact the prologue warns the audience to prepare for 'a sullen, tragic scene':

> If any spirit breathes within this round
> Uncapable of weighty passion . . .
> Who winks and shuts his apprehension up
> From common sense of what men were, and are,
> Who would not know what men must be – let such
> Hurry amain from our black-visag'd shows . . . (13-20)

'What men were, *and are*': the setting in an Italy of the past is not without relevance to the present time and place; 'what men *must be*': the course of action which the characters are driven to adopt in the play corresponds to the realities of life. This is very clear, and far from parody. Certainly there are touches of comic relief in the play, which amount to a kind of grim farce entirely compatible with an overall tragic effect. These are necessary precisely as safeguards against the pitfalls of child acting. They avoid, especially in the early scenes, the danger of unconscious anti-climax in the sustained rendering of tragic scenes by actors whose emotional range was naturally limited. Indeed the dialogue explicitly points up their limitations. 'I will not swell like a tragedian', declares the boy who acts Antonio (II.ii.105); and at the turning-point of the play the child actor who takes the part of old Pandulpho exclaims:

> Why, all this while I ha' but play'd a part
> Like to some boy that acts a tragedy,
> Speaks burly words and raves out passion;
> But when he thinks upon his infant weakness
> He drops his eye.   (IV. ii. 70–4)

No play designed as a parody would contain these quite unironical admissions of the shortcomings of tragedy as performed by children.

On the other hand, the tragic effect is strongly reinforced by Marston's classical sense of form. The action is tightly controlled without digressions, the scene being located throughout in the Venetian court and the time extending over exactly two days. The use of striking clocks, entries with torches or tapers, and frequent references to dawn, day-break, nightfall, sunshine and moonlight, mark the passing of the hours. Act I begins at exactly two a.m. with Piero's entry after the double murder in the two hours since midnight; at five Maria reaches the court; and Antonio later announces the coming of 'infant Morn'. The day is filled with the events of Act II until Mellida observes the rising of the moon. Act III, the emotional climax of the play, opens in 'Saint Mark's church' on the stroke of midnight and proceeds until the second dawn, during which time Andrugio's ghost rises, appears to his wife and son, and departs, as ghosts must, at sunrise. Act IV, the second day, brings the rallying of the revengers, and in Act V the catastrophic vengeance is consummated in the torchlight and revelry of the third night. The effect of this tight construction is to bring into sharp focus the basic conflicts of the play, in contrast to the deliberately blurred

[25]

vision of Shakespeare's *Hamlet*, with its unspecified lapses of time, its digressions and ambivalencies.

Marston leaves nothing uncertain. Piero is the type of all abominable tyrants, without any mitigating qualities of self-searching or remorse. His hypocritical poses, his crude self-congratulations are funny, as those of tyrants and demagogues are at all times in history, without being any the less terrible.[8] Like every dictator, he is uneasy in the presence of 'vinegar tart spirits'. His need is for sycophants and fools, not honest counsellors:

> He that's ambitious-minded and but man
> Must have his followers beasts, dubb'd slavish sots,
> Whose service is obedience and whose wit
> Reacheth no further than to admire their lord ... (II.i.53–6)

The state in fact requires that the people should not only endure but even cheer the rulers who oppress them:

> Our subjects not alone to bear, but praise our acts. (II.i.125)

How then should the virtuous man react to the evil of power? Antonio like Hamlet reads his book, which turns out to be the moral essays of Seneca, and ponders the aphorisms it contains. '*Ferte fortiter . . .*' 'Endure bravely; this is the thing in which thou surpassest God; for he is outside the sufferance of ills; you are above it.' But the complacent advice of philosophers brings no comfort; he throws the book aside impatiently. Pandulpho, a life-long Stoic, repeats the well-worn maxims of patience and endurance, only to break off suddenly and shed unphilosophic tears as he remembers his murdered son. He realises that all this while he has deceived himself with words: 'Man will break out, despite philosophy.' The alternative for both is action, the acceptance of revenge, with all the defilement that results from opposing evil to evil. Accordingly Antonio commits himself to the elemental urge of blood and satisfies the ghost's demand. His initial victim is the son of Piero, heir to the tyrant, but in himself an affectionate, entirely innocent boy. The murder of Julio is horrible not only in itself but in the casuistry with which Antonio justifies it and the black ritual of human sacrifice that ensues. But the private crime is only the first step to the public assassination of Piero. For this Antonio and Pandulpho join forces and enact the vengeance of the whole people. The tyrant's enormities have reached the point where they can no longer be endured by his subjects:

[26]

> The rumour's got 'mong troop of citizens,
> Making loud murmur with confused din.
> One shakes his head and sighs, 'O ill-used power!'
> Another frets and sets his grinding teeth,
> Foaming with rage, and swears this must not be.   (V.ii.43–7)

Again the murder, preluded by a masque, is performed with Senecan horrors as Piero's tongue is torn out, he is offered the flesh of his own son, and is finally killed – like Caesar at the Capitol – in a succession of ritual stabbings by all the conspirators. After the orgy the assassins are congratulated by the senators of Venice for their deed of liberation:

> Bless'd be you all; and may your honours live
> Religiously held sacred, even for ever and ever.   (V.iii.127–8)

They are offered honours and rewards. But Pandulpho, speaking for them all, renounces these. Too much has been suffered and enacted; too much has been learned.

> We know the world; and did we know no more
> We would not live to know ...   (V.iii.147–8)

Were it not forbidden 'by constraint of holy bands' they would put an end to their lives. As it is, they will spend the rest of their days 'In holy verge of some religious order, Most constant votaries' (152–3).

Literary scholars have not found much difficulty in pointing out the confused ethics and moral inconsistencies of this play. We may assume that Marston, who after a few years gave up writing for the stage and devoted the rest of his life to the church, was also aware of them. But he must also have known what happens to abstract principle, in life as well as in drama, at the point of crisis when action takes over from doctrine. In this connection we may look back again to Italian renaissance annals and consider the case of Olgiato and his companions. These three young patricians of Milan grew up under the dukedom of Galeazzo Maria Sforza, a ruler as lecherous and cruel as any Jacobean stage villain.[9] They were pious, God-fearing young men, devout sons of the church. But Olgiato's sister had been raped, and one of his companions robbed of his inheritance, under the workings of the regime. On the 26th of December 1476 they came early to St Stephen's church, received the sacrament, and prayed to the patron saint of their city, asking him to favour their designs and forgive them for what they had to do. As the Duke and his retinue entered the church, the three suddenly surrounded him and stabbed him to death. Two of them were killed on the spot; Olgiato had the misfortune to escape. After two days he was caught alive and, according the euphemism of the time, 'put to the question'. In spite of these torments, he refused to repent his deed, but declared that the offering of his life would be blessed by God and man. Stripped of his clothes, facing the executioner's sword, he spoke his last words in classical Latin: *Mors acerba, fama perpetua, stabit vetus memoria facti*. 'Cruel death, lasting fame; our deed will long be remembered.' At the time of his death he was twenty-three.[10]

If *Antonio's Revenge* includes those moral ambiguities that are part of the human condition, it is unequivocal in stating the facts of tyranny and political protest. The treatment is different in *The Revenger's Tragedy*, and it is not surprising that this play has called forth an extraordinary range of critical attitudes. Tourneur's vision of corruption has been seen by T. S. Eliot as immature in so far as it exceeded its object, and was therefore to be regarded as a projection from the poet's 'inner world of nightmare'; as such it was essentially 'a document on one human being, Tourneur'.[11] Since there is much doubt as to who in fact wrote the play, such a document would have to remain an eternally cryptic case-study of an unknown individual. L. G. Salingar, on the other hand, pointed out that the unrealistic presentation of characters and the stylized setting belonged less to a dream world than to the morality tradition, with its personifications of virtues and vices. As for the object of the poet's disgust, this was not fantasy, but 'the disintegration of a whole social order'.[12] Yet this view too has been qualified by those who note the uncertainties of tone, the triteness of some of the sententious comments, and above all, the cynical zest of Vindice the protagonist, who often becomes imaginatively identified with the corruption he attacks.[13] Again, it has been suggested that this very unevenness is a virtue, in that it creates a sense of detachment from events on stage, while fostering a profounder awareness of reality through ironies and grotesque effects.

None of these attitudes should, I think, be altogether disregarded. Whoever wrote *The Revenger's Tragedy* possessed a hyperacute and very individual sensibility, kindled by a somewhat *voyeur* interest in perverse sexuality, cruelty, self-abandon and decay. But this interest was only spasmodic; there is an equal readiness to fall back on well-worn dramatic convention. Sometimes there is a return to the manner of the morality play or Tudor interlude; sometimes an echoing of Jacobean modes; sometimes what seems to us an anticipation of modern black farce. But perhaps the most useful approach to the play is the most obvious: to see it in the first instance as a variant of the revenge tragedy of the time. That is surely how its original audience must have received it; and its distinctive qualities must have shown up all the more clearly against this norm.

As a revenge tragedy the play is immediately familiar. There is the Italian court setting and a story which in essentials undoubtedly harks back to the historical assassination of Duke Alessandro of Florence in 1537 – the source, quite independently, of de Musset's *Lorenzaccio*.[14] History and dramatic convention are brought into a single focus. There is the tyrant ruler, slave to his own passions, the fount of corruption and sin in a whole society. Against him is set the anti-type Vindice, the revenger, brooding over a dead father and a violated mistress. The play develops the moral contrast between the family of the tyrant and the family of the revenger, the testing of virtue and integrity, and in a second wave of vengeance, a bloody consummation through the usual device of a festive masque. In dramatic terms the immediate precedent is probably *Antonio's Revenge*; but there is a further satirical dimension which takes over elements from Marston's later tragicomedy *The Malcontent* and which also owes something to Shakespeare's *Hamlet*. Vindice, like Antonio, is melancholy, passionate and embittered; however, like Malevole in *The Malcontent*, and like Hamlet too, he has the second *persona* of the satirist and cynic as he moves in disguise amongst his enemies. As in these plays, the revenge theme is complicated by a tangle of secondary intrigues and punctuated by general diatribes and moralizing soliloquies. Within these limits, *The Revenger's Tragedy* presents no problems. But what must have struck the first spectators of this play, accustomed to revenge drama of the time, is that all these qualities are transformed by being set in a changed perspective. The hard secular outlines of Renaissance political drama are dissolved by a moral impressionism belonging to the timeless folk vision of men in high places. Life and affairs at court are not seen from within, but judged as they appear from below-stairs, from the street, from rumour and report, where they present a monstrous affront to all popular conceptions of human behaviour. Although, as I have said, Tourneur's plot has striking resemblances to events in the Florence of 1537, in the play these are abstracted from any political or historical context. The Duke rules over an unnamed state in a vague, unspecified Italy. Tyrant as he is, he makes no mention of territorial ambitions, nor does he plan to dominate other polities. Warfare, diplomacy, treaties, alliances do not enter into the considerations of court. Power means only unlimited scope for the satisfaction of desire, chiefly the physical

desires of gluttony and lechery. What the palace offers as its principal
rewards are not so much offices and honours as

> stirring meats,
> Ready to move out of the dishes, that
> E'en now quicken when they're eaten;
> Banquets abroad by torchlight, music, sports, . . .
> Nine coaches waiting – hurry, hurry, hurry.   (II.i.200 ff.)

Delicious food, sexual excitement, hectic movement: these are seen as
the preoccupations of the great; significantly the comment after 'hurry,
hurry' is 'Ay, to the devil'. Spurio the Duke's bastard sees his very
existence as the accidental result of a lascivious orgy:

> I was begot
> After some gluttonous dinner, some stirring dish
> Was my first father, when deep healths went round,
> And ladies' cheeks were painted red with wine,
> Their tongues as short and nimble as their heels,
> Uttering words sweet and thick; and when they rose,
> Were merrily disposed to fall again . . .   (I.ii.180–6)[15]

Unlike Marston's gallery of well-observed court characters in *The
Malcontent* – painted old ladies, pompous time-servers, cunning bawds
– these figures are hardly more than personifications of vice, as their
names – Lussurioso, Ambitioso, Supervacuo and so on – imply. The
political abuses of despotism count for less than the sinfulness it pro-
motes; the words 'devil', 'hell', 'damnation' are constantly recurrent.
Sin is at once attractive and monstrous, fascinating and repulsive, so
that interest is sustained in the Duke with his senile lust; the Duchess,
incestuously seducing her husband's bastard son; Lussurioso, heir to
the throne, with his compulsive indiscriminating desires; an entire
family motivated only by its perverse rivalries.

This overlaying of the themes of revenge tragedy amounts to a return to the popular morality tradition, with its castigation of evil
amongst the great ones of this world. But instead of presenting an un-
changing reality, *The Revenger's Tragedy* is acutely responsive to the
contemporary scene. Italy as the cradle of despotism may be left in the
shadows, but Jacobean England makes up a lurid picture of waste and
corruption, in which wealth and fertility are being squandered away
by spendthrift heirs, the new rich, and noblemen turned courtiers.
Patrimonies are 'washed a-pieces', 'fruitfields turned into bastards'.
Estates are sold to pay for the fantastic extravagance of court dress:

Lands that were mete by the rod, that labour's spared,
Tailors ride down, and measure 'em by the yard;
Fair trees, those comely foretops of the field,
Are cut to maintain head-tires . . .   (II.i.223-6)[16]

Usurers flourish, while the common people are ruined by the endless
processes of the law. The abuses were not new, but their effects had
been speeded up by a galloping inflation and a growing parasitism
which had eroded all established positions and values, leading, in Salingar's words, to 'the disintegration of a whole social order'. For the
author of the play and, one supposes, most of his audience, the political–
economic factors were not well understood. What they plainly saw
was that the normal processes of nature and human nature had broken
down. Society seemed to breed monsters on high and a proliferation of
vice through every rank. While therefore morality techniques were
applied to depict the sinfulness and injustice of the world, they served
only a negative function and had no positive guidance to offer.

The loss of positive values influences in turn the structure of the
play. There is no norm of a virtuous polity against which the Duke's
régime can be offset; no supposition that a good ruler has been overthrown or murdered before the action began; no appearance of an
uncorrupted heir to take over the injured state. The Duke's family are
all cut of the same cloth, bastard or legitimate, younger son or elder.
Behind them, it is implied, stands a long line of corrupt rulers reaching
back into the past. The lodge where the Duke is lured to his death is
also the place of assignation for his Duchess and Spurio, and was before
their time 'guilty Of his forefathers' lusts, and great folks' riots'. As
against these 'great folks', the impoverished family of Vindice, his
brother Hippolito, his sister Castiza and their mother Gratiana cannot
promise any alternative form of rule; at most they provide a contrast
between the honesty and chastity of the people and the vices of their
superiors. But even this contrast is questionable. Vindice in his courtier's
disguise has little difficulty in tempting his mother to the point where
she is willing to make her own daughter 'a drab of state, a cloth of silver
slut'. She later repents; but her vulnerability is in keeping with the
play's pervading cynicism about the virtue of women. As for Vindice
and his accomplice Hippolito, there is a marked ambivalence about
their moral position. They play their parts with unmistakable relish as
pimps and go-betweens. The indignation they voice is blended with
delight in their own ingenious cunning; and they often become merged
with their assumed personalities.

In this moral confusion Marston's carefully drawn pattern of retribution becomes obscure. No supernatural powers function in *The Revenger's Tragedy*, as they do in *Antonio's Revenge* and other plays in the Senecan tradition. There is no ghost or fury to actuate vengeance. The skull in Vindice's hand shows the presence of death amid the silk and silver of court; it is even the instrument of death in Act III; but it has no celestial or infernal will of its own. Even the thunder and shooting star merely register passive approval of Vindice's actions. Heaven may like the tragedy, but does not produce it. Vindice makes his own drama; Vindice provides his own values. In *Antonio's Revenge* the authority of the wise Stoic Pandulpho was needed to justify action against tyranny; in *The Malcontent* the satirist-revenger Malevole is the true Duke Altofronto in disguise. Tourneur's play begins by suggesting a similar collaboration of wisdom with energy. In Act I the old courtier Antonio, whose wife has been ravished by the Duchess's youngest son, takes a solemn oath to avenge her death. An alliance is to be expected between him and Vindice. Instead, the theme is forgotten and Vindice acts alone. His oscillations between passionate diatribes against vice and joyous participation in the intrigues of court, between laments for his lost mistress and trite aphorisms on women's follies, between Hamlet-like meditations on the vanity of life and sadistic enactments of murder, make him the villain as well as the hero of his own play. When at last he over-reaches himself, carried away by his own cleverness, it is the same courtier Antonio, his vow of revenge forgotten, who orders his arrest.

Critics whose main object is to trace moral patterns in tragedy are put to grave contortions in discussing this play. Here is a revenge drama without political perspectives, a morality without positive standards. What is all too easily overlooked is that a puzzling text read in libraries may assume unity in diversity when acted on the living stage. This is the case with *The Revenger's Tragedy* as performed by the Royal Shakespeare Company at Stratford and recently in London. The interpretation is of course contemporary; we are made to see the play almost exclusively in the spirit of modern black farce. There are some modish additions that only serve to distract. But more importantly, in the evoking of a contemporary response new insights are gained. The nihilism of our own age, sprung of a sense of helplessness in a world controlled by huge aggregations of power, has its affinities to folk attitudes in other times. In the theatre, before a present-day audience, *The Revenger's Tragedy*, with its discrepancies of tone, its mingling of indignation and farce, frustration and contempt, triteness and grotesquery, takes on coherence and point. It is likely that the response at its first performance was not dissimilar. The spectacle of the court, caricatured, degenerate, pullulating with intrigue, would mirror the secret attitude of the people down the ages towards the powers that be, recognizing in them qualities at once horrific, fascinating, and funny; an attitude which, out of a conviction of helplessness resembling our own, of necessity tempers hatred with laughter. Even Vindice's moral ambivalence may have established a *rapport* with the Jacobean audience, as it does with audiences today. In the popular tradition the Vice was a well-loved figure, with his japes at the expense of authority; though in the end, of course, conventional virtue triumphed. The outlaw, the railroad bandit, the bank robber, belong to the same category of folk-heroes, and Vindice is a member of the club. Unavoidably he is rounded up with his brother, after bringing off the total revenge of his dreams. It is in the nature of things that Antonio, instead of joining him, should rally in the end to the cause of authority and the older generation. But Vindice goes unrepentant to his execution, justified in his own eyes, and undoubtedly in the eyes of the audience:

> We have enough, i'faith;
> We're well, our mother turn'd, our sister true;
> We die after a nest of dukes. Adieu!   (V.iii.123-5)

NOTES

1. G. K. Hunter, 'English Folly and Italian Vice: John Webster', *Jacobean Theatre*, ed. J. R. Brown and Bernard Harris, Stratford-upon-Avon Studies (1960); reprinted in *John Webster, A Critical Anthology*, ed G. K. and S. K. Hunter (1969), p. 262.

2. *The Complete Works of John Webster*, ed. F. L. Lucas (1927, 1966), I, p. 92. The remark should be read in its context (pp. 91-3), discussing an essay of Vernon Lee in 1884 which argued 'that all the Italian tragedies of the Elizabethans without exception are travesties of the truth, because there was not really anything tragic in cinquecento Italy.'

3. Macchiavelli, *Historia Fiorentina*, lib. VI, ch. 2; Ghirardacci, *Della Historia di Bologna* (1669), II, p. 127; Muratori, *Annali d'Italia* (1753), Vol. IX (1) xlii, p. 82; Sismondi, *Histoire des Républiques Italiennes du Moyen Age* (1826), IX, pp. 224-6. For accounts in English see J. A. Symonds, *The Renaissance in Italy* (1880), Vol. I, pp. 93-6, 118; Cecilia

M. Ady, *The Bentivoglio of Bologna* (1937), pp. 28–30. Popular risings against despots, raising the cry of '*Viva la libertà!*' and calling for a return to free institutions, recurred sporadically throughout the fifteenth century, in 1411 at Bologna, in 1412 at Milan, in 1435 at Genoa, in 1445 at Bologna, in 1457 at Milan, in 1488 at Forli; culminating in the three-year siege of the republic of Florence by the armies of Spain and the Empire, 1527–30.

4. *The Moral Vision of Jacobean Tragedy*, p. 152.

5. T. S. Eliot, 'John Marston' (1934), in *Elizabethan Dramatists* (1963), p. 154.

6. Cf. Seneca, *De Remediis Fortuitorum: Mors, exilium, luctus, dolor, non sunt supplicia sed tributa vivendi. Neminem illaesum fata transmittit . . . omnes consequentur.*

7. R. A. Foakes, 'John Marston's Fantastical Plays: *Antonio and Mellida* and *Antonio's Revenge*', *Philological Quarterly* XLI (1962), pp. 229–39.

8. Compare the antics of Charlie Chaplin in *The Great Dictator* and of Brecht's protagonist in *The Resistible Rise of Arturo Ui*. Present-day parallels are not hard to find.

9. 'Galeazzo Maria Sforza . . . was full of avarice and malice, a false friend, and wholly unscrupulous in the gratification of his lusts . . . no woman was safe from his advances, and he took a particular pleasure in boasting of his successes to injured husbands and the members of dishonoured houses; once won or forced, his newest mistress was given over to his lackeys, and many a rich subject was made to gratify his greed for gold, or buried alive, or tortured to death.' Sismondi, *op. cit.*, translated William Boulting (1906), p. 619.

10. The story of Olgiato and his fellow conspirators is told in Corio, *Historia di Milano* (1503, ed. 1857), III part 6, ch. 3; Macchiavelli, *Historia Fiorentina*, VII ch. 6; Ripamonti, *Historia Mediolani* (1641–8), I, lib. vi, 449–56. For accounts in English, see Macchiavelli, *The Florentine History*, translated Thomas Bedingfeld (1595), Tudor Translations (1905), pp. 367–71; J. A. Symonds, *op. cit.*, I, 129–31; L. Collison-Morley, *The Story of the Sforzas* (1933), pp. 113–19.

11. T. S. Eliot, 'Tourneur' (1930), in *Elizabethan Dramatists*, p. 116.

12. L. G. Salingar, '*The Revenger's Tragedy* and the Morality Tradition', *Scrutiny* VI (1938), pp. 402–24; reprinted in *Elizabethan Drama*, ed. Kaufmann, pp. 208–24.

13. See T. B. Tomlinson, 'The Morality of Revenge: Tourneur's Critics', *Essays in Criticism* X (1960), pp. 134–47.

14. De Musset based his play on Benedetto Varchi's account, *Storia Fiorentina* lib. xv. (See Paul Dimoff, *La Genèse de Lorenzaccio*, Paris, 1936.) *The*

Revenger's Tragedy shows a considerable knowledge of the same historical episode, though modified for dramatic purposes. Like the real Lorenzino, Vindice acts as a procurer. Both have a widowed mother (in life, Maria Soderini), who is deceived by the part her son plays; both have a chaste and beautiful sister, who steadfastly refuses to become a court mistress (to Duke Alessandro in fact; to Lussurioso in the play). The murder of the Duke took place at a secret rendezvous; Lorenzino's accomplice was the criminal Scoroconcolo, Vindice's, his brother Hippolito. Alessandro's death, like that of Tourneur's Duke, was at first undiscovered; it was kept secret, and he was buried without religious rites. In Varchi's account, followed by de Musset, the Duke is lured to Lorenzino's house in the belief that he will meet there Lorenzino's aunt: G. F. Young, *The Medici* (1909), I, 506–10, relates the affair, mentioning that in fact the Duke was promised Lorenzino's sister. Her name was Laudomia; she was a celebrated beauty, whose portrait hangs in the Accademia delle Belle Arti in Florence. The historical background of *The Revenger's Tragedy* was pointed out by N. W. Bawcutt in *Notes and Queries* CXCVII (1957), 192–3, and Pierre Legouis in *Études Anglaises* XII (1959), pp. 47–55. R. A. Foakes in his edition of *The Revenger's Tragedy*, The Revels Plays (1966), pp. xxv–xxvi, assumes that Tourneur's source was Marguerite de Navarre's *Heptameron*, nov. 12, 2nd day, translated by Painter in *The Palace of Pleasure* (Foakes, Appendix I, pp. 131–5). But though based on the same historical event, this account could not have provided the material for the play. The Duke of Florence is sentimentalized, nothing is said of his assassin's long-premeditated design or activities as a procurer, and except for the murder itself, the story is sketchy. Clearly Tourneur had more direct access to the historical facts.

15. Tourneur scarcely exaggerates in his picture of court life under James I. Meals regularly consisted of twenty-four dishes, when the King and Queen were present; at least thirty on special occasions. High courtiers followed suit. The fashion had grown up of the 'ante-supper', where the board was covered as high as a tall man with choice dishes on view as the guests entered, then removed and replaced with fresh hot dishes for the meal itself. Occasions of drunken disorder were not infrequent at banquets and masques, when tables were overturned and quantities of food wasted. Sexual promiscuity was widespread. The court was frequented by procuresses such as Lady Grisby, notorious panders like Dr. Lamb, who arranged assignations at Brainford or Ware, and charlatans dealing in aphrodisiacs and abortions. (See Akrigg, *Jacobean Pageant*, chapters 14, 18.) Prostitutes ranged 'from court laundresses ready to earn sixpence, the minimum rate, in a dark corner, to highly expensive courtesans such as Venetia Stanley, one of the most beautiful woman of the age' (*ibid.*, p. 241). Bastards were openly acknowledged, and could be legitimized by

'rehabilitation' in default of legitimate heirs. Spurio, like Shakespeare's Edmund, was a familiar court figure of the age.

16. Akrigg mentions gowns for court ladies costing fifty Jacobean pounds to the yard for embroidering, and refers to the outlay of fourteen thousand pounds for hanging the lying-in chamber of the Countess of Salisbury with white satin embroidered with gold, or silver and pearl (pp. 228–9). Cf. *Vindice*: How go things at court? *Hippolito*: In silk and silver, brother: never braver (I.i.52–3).

III

Chapman:
The *Bussy* Plays

The revenge plays I have spoken about take as their theme an act of revolt against a tyrant or a tyrannical order. In Chapman's *Bussy D'Ambois* and its sequel *The Revenge of Bussy*, the central concern is less with an action than with a man. Bussy and Clermont, the protagonists, are both conceived on a heroic scale. In the dedication to his translation of the *Odyssey*, Chapman distinguished what he saw as the essential qualities of Homer's two epics:

> In one, Predominant Perturbation; in the other, over-ruling Wisedome: in one, the Bodie's fervour and fashion of outward Fortitude to all possible height of Heroicall Action; in the other, the Mind's inward, constant and unconquerd Empire, unbroken, unalterd with any most insolent and tyrannous infliction.[1]

Ennis Rees, in his book on Chapman's tragedies, relates these comments to Achilles and Odysseus, the respective heroes of the *Iliad* and *Odyssey*, and remarks that what might be called the Achilles type – perturbation, fortitude, action – is applicable to Bussy, and the Odysseus type – the mind's inward empire, unchanged by tyranny – to Clermont.[2] The comparison is helpful, but I cannot accept the inference drawn, that Chapman's two heroes are presented as object-lessons, one negative, the other positive; one demonstrating the evils of passion, the other the virtues of reason.[3] We have already met this polarity of types in the revenge plays, where the passionate rebel and the quietist philosopher reflect alternative reactions to the tyranny that oppresses them both. The roots of evil are not in themselves, but in the world they inhabit. Both Hieronymo and Hamlet experience the conflicting urges to acquiescence and revolt; Pandulpho and Andrugio, who present contrasted attitudes, ultimately join forces against the common foe. The polarity goes back to Seneca, whose Stoic dissent found expression both in the philosophical man of the Moral Essays and the titanic rebels of the Tragedies.[4] It is not without significance that Chapman makes his contrasted heroes brothers. Bussy and Clermont alike stand above the height of common men. In their courage or their consistency, their passion or their rationality, they claim an inherent right to judge rather than be judged, to decide the merits of laws and the rulers who make them, since the essence of justice and kingship lies in themselves. For all their self-assurance, they are undone by forces they cannot master, and the conflict results in tragedy. In a sense, this might be called revenge tragedy in reverse, where the revenge is taken not by the challenger of the order but by the order itself, exercising its built-in sanctions against the man who defies it. Like Seneca's Hercules even more than Homer's Achilles, like Seneca himself even more than Odysseus, Chapman's historical heroes are crushed by the antagonism of the powers that be.

Let us consider first the earlier play, *Bussy D'Ambois*. The story was drawn straight from life: the hectic, violent, colourful life of a French courtier and nobleman born in 1549, at eighteen a military commander, in his twenties a favourite of Monsieur, the brother and heir-presumptive to the king. Notorious for his prowess, his quarrels, his duels, his amours, Bussy was killed at the age of thirty by the enraged husband whose wife he had seduced when he was commander in Anjou. Bussy's exploits were almost legendary in his time, and in the nineteenth century they provided material for a novel by Dumas. Here was a character who called for dramatic treatment: the question was, what interpretation should be given to such a life. Had Chapman wished, he could have followed the precedent of his friend Marlowe and created a kind of stage epic rather after the fashion of *Tamburlaine*, spreading the action over the many years and varied settings of Bussy's career and highlighting the plentiful opportunities it afforded – the battles, the duels, the sexual conquests – that made up his hero's adult life. Instead, he chose to compress the action within an almost classical span of two days. Only very brief intervals elapse between the five acts, and events are centred upon the French court, where nothing more remarkable is taking place than games of chess and light conversation. The duel fought by six noblemen, of whom Bussy alone survived, is reported by messenger; the love affair with Tamyra which leads to his death is only implied between the staging of his first meeting with her and his departure in the morning. Nor is this compression due mainly to a pedantic respect for classical form: Chapman shows himself the master, not the slave of traditional rules. While Bussy's physical exploits are subordinated to the wider issues they involve, the process by which Bussy is

destroyed, occupying the second half of the play, is dramatized with all
the effects the Jacobean theatre placed at Chapman's disposal: the use
of trap-doors, arras, and gallery above stage; the simultaneous
presentation of two locations; the conjuring up of spirits; disguises,
bloodshed, sword-fights, and pistol-shots. More important than either
classical precedent or popular audience appeal was the need to express
the primary tragic theme: the defeat of the hero and the forces he
stands for.

Here the question arises: what is the meaning of this defeat? It has
become increasingly fashionable in academic criticism to extrapolate
from Elizabethan drama a moral order, or a moral vision, which is
thought to have been the playwright's main concern in his honorary
capacity as Christian humanist. Marlowe's *Tamburlaine* is explicated as
a morality play designed to impress audiences with the spectacle of
divine punishment; Shakespeare's *Antony and Cleopatra* becomes an
object-lesson in the sin of sexuality and the wantonness of counting the
Roman empire well lost for love.[5] Tragedies are unravelled as studies
in theology, heroes are identified with saints, or Christ-figures in disguise. The medieval ethos marches on through the seventeenth century
until in the year 1642 it tumbles into the ditch of the English Revolution.
This neo-pietism, in which one may at times suspect a recoil from sub-
versive currents of our own day, hardly affects the responses of audiences and readers outside academic circles. Shakespeare and Marlowe
speak out for themselves. Chapman, however, calls for some defence.
The professional stage has not yet rediscovered his plays, and Victorian
assessments of him still linger on, suggesting a worthy but dull philosophical poet with little sense of the theatre he wrote for. It is easy,
therefore, to reduce his tragic themes to a set of moral attitudes which
Chapman (and for that matter all other Jacobean dramatists) was supposed to uphold. According to the most rigid of these interpretations,
Bussy D'Ambois is a cautionary lesson in the operation of society's just
laws when challenged by pride and passion. Bussy, as 'one of the bestial
servants of self-love', richly deserves his fall.[6] The praises showered
upon him in the course of the play must be read as irony, including the
king's choric comment describing Bussy as 'a man so good, that only
would uphold Man in his native noblesse'; including, too, the virtual
apotheosis of him near the end, where he is addressed as 'brave relics of
a complete man' and acclaimed as a new star in the firmament. A more
flexible approach welcomes the play not as a moral exemplum but
rather as a philosophical tragedy on the uselessness of man's endeavours

in a world fallen through original sin.[7] Chapman, it is implied, took the fall of Adam on the first day of his creation as the reason for all oppression and injustice by man and fate down the intervening ages to the reign of King James I. One might wonder what compelling force urged Chapman to write a contemporary play for the demonstration of this negative doctrine. But in fact *Bussy D'Ambois* contains no reference to original sin. What the play does have a good deal to say about is the decline in natural virtue since an earlier age when there were neither rulers nor private property,

> Nor had the full impartial hand of Nature,
> That all things gave in her original,
> Without these definite terms of Mine and Thine,
> Been turn'd unjustly to the hand of Fortune ...   (III.ii.98–101)

This points to a secular theory of history based on a belief in the goodness of natural man, which serves to reinforce the strictures of Greville, Alexander and others on the corrupt society of their time, not to show the futility of all aspiration since the fall of Adam. Yet another critical approach, bewildered by the incompatibility between Chapman's morals and the contradictory character of his hero, sees the play as one in which the author 'muddled his high design' in trying to reconcile Stoic ethics with Machiavellian relativism.[8]

In my opinion, *Bussy D'Ambois* deserves to be considered first and foremost not as an exposition of moral or philosophical beliefs but as a tragedy functioning in its own terms. It is a difficult play, bristling with paradoxes and contradictions, not unlike the metaphysical poetry of the age. And like the metaphysical poem, it is a work of art, not a statement of doctrine. Had *Bussy* been a rather muddled philosophical statement dressed up for the theatre, it would not have been performed again and again until nearly the end of the seventeenth century, with some of the best actors of the time in its leading parts. As a tragedy, not a morality play or a thesis. *Bussy* is primarily an exploration of human conflicts, which involve, but do not merely serve to illustrate, opposed attitudes and principles. Concepts, ideals, moral absolutes are issues bound up with men's lives; but in drama their validity is existential; they are shaped, dissolved, contradicted or modified in the process of living. This is true even if we consider the abstractions which are evoked in *Bussy D'Ambois*, instead of applying to the play such moral schemes as we might like it to exemplify. Nature, Fortune, Fate, Virtue, Nobility, are terms very much in evidence in the reflections, comments and dialogue. Their connotations, however, shift back and forth with the sweep of dramatic conflict and rarely provide a satisfactory explanation of what actually takes place. This is not a sign of the author's confusion but an indication of what happens of necessity to ideas in action. What remains constant is the inner dynamic of the tragedy itself, the inherent opposition between the hero and his society.

The play opens with a statement of the issues in abstract terms.

> Fortune, not Reason, rules the state of things,
> Reward goes backward, Honour on his head;
> Who is not poor is monstrous . . .

This is spoken by Bussy, who enters alone, described in the stage direction as 'poor' and no doubt showing his poverty by the costume he wears. The setting is a 'green retreat' symbolical of the world of nature. Gradually in his monologue the abstractions become more definite as he elaborates the simile of great men as 'colossic statues', vulgarly impressive but hollow inside, or as seamen whose 'tall ships richly built' can only be brought into harbour by some 'poor staid fisherman'. At last Monsieur enters, dressed as befits his high rank, escorted by two pages, to provide the visual embodiment of Bussy's imagery. His object is to draw Bussy from his green retreat into the world of state, from 'obscure abodes' into the bright light of political eminence. Although the drift of Bussy's monologue has been the vanity of greatness and the virtue of withdrawal from society, he nevertheless answers Monsieur's call:

> I am for honest actions, not for great,
> If I may bring up a new fashion
> And rise in Court for virtue, speed his plough . . .   (I.i.128–30)

From now on, the action proceeds through a series of particular encounters wherein Bussy's reaction to the follies and presumptions of society express themselves not in general reflections but in concrete behaviour. The first encounter is with Maffé, Monsieur's steward, in his chain and velvet jacket, whose supercilious bearing and attempt to cheat Bussy of the gold his master has sent earns him a box on the ears. In the next scene Bussy, self-conscious in his newly acquired court dress, refuses to show deference to the Duchess of Guise and speaks to her before her husband in the light, indecent tones a man might use to a prostitute. The Duke of Guise is furious, but Bussy stands his ground and only the King's presence prevents the quarrel from turning into armed combat. Guise's side is taken by the languid courtiers who gibe

[41]

at Bussy's dress and bearing in tones of easy contempt:

> We held discourse of a perfumed ass, that being disguised in
> a lion's case, imagined himself a lion: I hope that touched
> not you.   (I.ii.206–8)

When Bussy retorts with a violent threat, Barrisor calls to the others in mock-trepidation: 'For life's sake let's be gone; he'll kill's outright else' (212). The remark is fully prophetic. While the steward was merely cuffed for his impertinence and the Duchess insulted for her haughty bearing the sneers of Barrisor and his companions cost them their lives.

These details have been dwelt on to emphasize the way the drama functions on two levels: through immediate dramatic impressions as well as through the interplay of such polarities as fortune and reason, nature and artifice, appearance and reality. Bussy's killing of the courtiers is justified in front of the King as a noble act in defence of his fame, a quality more precious than life. But Bussy himself extends this into a claim to stand by right of nature above both King and Law:

> since I am free,
> (Offending no just law), let no law make
> By any wrong it does, my life her slave;
> When I am wrong'd, and that law fails to right me,
> Let me be king myself (as man was made),
> And do a justice that exceeds the law ...   (II.i.194–9)

Now between the two levels of action and concept there is an evident discrepancy. Bussy, the apostle of virtue and nature, behaves in society with an impetuosity and violence which results in the death of five men sacrificed on the altar of his 'fame'. His behaviour was not in fact extraordinary. Between 1601 and 1609, the year when Chapman was writing his tragedies, some two thousand French noblemen died fighting duels in defence of their honour.[9] But such recklessness, however common in its age, was a far cry from the principles of natural virtue as either Christian or Stoic might understand these. Bussy's conduct was not so much that of the noble savage as of the savage nobleman, upholding in the age of the Renaissance an outworn feudal code. By the end of the second act, moreover, he has added adultery to his exploits by seducing a married woman, the wife of Count Montsurry, in furtherance of the natural man's right to freedom of love. Again it is an action more in keeping with the medieval code of courtly love, championed with defiance in a society proclaiming the sanctity of marriage.

Understandably, these discrepancies have worried critics who like to see Jacobean drama as the articulation of certain moral concepts. It is not, of course, impossible or unlikely that Chapman had in mind some scheme of moral values when he began to write *Bussy D'Ambois*. But whatever his intention may have been, his creative talent ensured that the scheme became in the course of writing not so much 'muddled' as transformed. Drama, like life, depends on a fruitful tension between principles and actions. In society, in the political world, men seek justification for their conduct in ideals, myths, doctrines, ideologies, which have only a tangential relevance to their immediate aims. These mental constructs nevertheless give to their deeds a significance beyond the limits of the historical moment. Chapman's Bussy behaves in fact like a dissident nobleman of the age, seeking to assert his traditional freedom of action in a changed society increasingly centralized and regulated by the state and its functionaries. He will defend his honour at the point of the sword – in an age of legalism and gunpowder. He will uphold his right to engage in chivalric romance – in a society which requires marriage, though permitting casual lechery. But he does so in the name of man's natural freedom and virtue, a prerogative which kings and their laws have usurped. This is indeed the way men must relate action to thought, unless they are to abdicate their human dignity and become, like Monsieur, mere politicians and time-servers. Accordingly Bussy's defiance acquires a timeless validity. His insistence on the inherent rights of man relates him to the republicans of antiquity, Brutus and Cassius. It looks ahead to the stand of John Lilburne and his Levellers in the English Revolution that lay forty years ahead.[10] It gives him affinities with the French revolutionary Danton in the seventeen-nineties and the Ukrainian anarchist Makhno in the nineteen-twenties; turbulent men all of them, who failed in their historical period but have their place in the collective memory of humanity.

By leaving his 'green retreat', Bussy enters the world of inverted values. Here passive virtue can no longer be cultivated: its activation requires in itself an inversion that will oppose the essence to the outward form. In beating the supercilious steward, a nonentity in a chain of office, Bussy is affirming the equality of man. In talking bawdy to the Duchess of Guise he exposes the vulgarity of the court lady under her trappings of rank. His angry challenge to the titters of the courtiers asserts true nobility against sham. And his seduction of Tamyra defies the hypocritical sexual morality which her husband follows when he advises her to tolerate the princely philandering of Monsieur:

[43]

> Pray thee, bear with him.
> Thou know'st he is a bachelor and a courtier,
> Ay, and a prince ...
> That prince doth high in virtue's reckoning stand
> That will entreat a vice and not command.   (II.ii.68–70, 74–5)

In Busy's secret courtship his agent and go-between is the Friar, surely the most unfriarly friar in Renaissance drama. On the face of it, his behaviour is simply that of a pander. Yet he performs his office with all the gravity and devoutness of a holy man, and is treated as such by both Bussy and Tamyra. Again, formal morality is negated in the recovery of its essence. In his devotion to Tamyra's welfare, the Friar ignores the practice of his order, which would in effect make him the watchdog of her unloved husband. He brings her peace; but it is the physical peace of nature, the calming by love of the storm raised in her blood, not the peace of the spirit he might be expected to further.[11] Yet in terms of the drama this rejection of traditional ethics becomes an affirmation when seen in contrast to the murderous mission of the false friar, Montsurry in disguise, who violates both physical and spiritual peace as he carries the letter written in Tamyra's blood that will bring Bussy to his death. With extraordinary daring Chapman presents calming of blood outside the marriage bond as a positive virtue when set against the shedding of blood in the enforcement of that bond.

But the Friar is more than a lovers' go-between. He is also the intermediary between them and a realm of dark truth that is inaccessible to the daylight consciousness of the world of state. Asked by Bussy to use his 'skill in the command of good aerial spirits' the Friar unexpectedly calls up the infernal power Behemoth. The situation is superficially like that of Faustus and Mephistophilis; according to theatrical tradition such forbidden conjuring should reveal in no uncertain fashion the evil and ugliness of hell. Yet Behemoth appears as a beautiful and dignified figure. Complaining of the 'accursed light' into which he has risen, he styles himself

> Emperor
> Of that inscrutable darkness where are hid
> All deepest truths, and secrets never seen.   (IV.ii.67–9)

Eugene Waith in his fine book *The Herculean Hero* has brought out very clearly the significance of the idea of darkness in Chapman's thought, and the function of images of darkness in this play. Tamyra's beautiful invocation of night while awaiting Bussy dwells on its properties of magic, its power to 'Make the violent wheels Of Time and Fortune stand' (II.ii.115–16). At the beginning of the play Bussy 'Neglects the light and loves obscure abodes'; he is called by Monsieur into the corrupted light of greatness. Night is, in Waith's words, 'peaceful and strong, a guide to virtuous conduct, a source of poetic inspiration, and a storehouse of learning'.[12] Behemoth, instead of being the conventional fiend, the enemy to man, appears in Chapman's play as the friend of man in his passional nature, guardian of the deepest truths, a figure who calls to mind the 'dark gods' of ancient mysteries, not the devil of Christian tradition.

Yet in the tragedy of Bussy neither Behemoth nor any other superhuman agency can change the course of events. All they can do is to extend Bussy's knowledge of the truth; they can advise and warn; but they have no control over men's fate or fortune. Nor have these very terms, fate and fortune, any of the divine properties accorded to them in classical drama. For Chapman and his audiences, they are no more than personified abstractions. Like nature and virtue, the concepts serve to endow the dramatic action with a more than immediate significance. It is in this sense that we should understand Bussy's question 'Who are Fate's ministers?' and Behemoth's reply, 'The Guise and Monsieur' (V.iii.63–4). Bussy is not led to his downfall by fate; at all times he has a free choice. The Guise and Monsieur are indeed the only fates of the play, the only real agents of the tragedy. It is when these two eminences join forces that the revenge of state upon the rebellious individual is fulfilled.

Bussy has entered the political world hoping to 'bring up a new fashion And rise at court for virtue'. His killing of Barrisor and the other courtiers does him no harm, since he is defended at that time by Monsieur. Nor would his adultery with Tamyra have led to ill consequences had it not been exploited by the Guise. It is when Bussy attempts to put into practice his plan for reform that his downfall is assured. He offers his services to Henri III as the king's 'hawk' to hunt down the corrupters of society:

> Show me a great man . . . That by his greatness
> Bombasts his private roofs with public riches . . .
> Show me a clergyman, that is in voice
> A lark of heaven, in heart a mole of earth,
> That hath good living, and a wicked life . . .
> Show me a lawyer that turns sacred law . . .
> Into a harpy, that eats all but's own . . .   (III.ii.25–54 *passim*)

Where, asks the Guise suspiciously, will these be found ? Bussy replies, 'I'll hawk about your house for one of them.' This is enough; as soon as the king has left, the Guise conspires with Monsieur for Bussy's over-throw. Neither of them as yet knows of his affair with Tamyra, but once Tamyra's maid betrays her mistress's secret, the trap is set. Mont-surry's jealousy is aroused, and Tamyra is brutally forced into the part of decoy.

In this tragic hunt the Guise and Monsieur destroy their prey. Guise, a man of blood, knows only mindless violence. It is Monsieur the politi-cian whose brain and cunning direct the operation. Monsieur's full significance is brought out in the set speech of Bussy which closes Act III.

> I think
> That y'are for perjuries the very prince
> Of all intelligencers; and your voice
> Is like an eastern wind, that where it flies
> Knits nets of caterpillars, with which you catch
> The prime of all the fruits that kingdom yields;
> That your political head is the curs'd fount
> Of all the violence, rapine, cruelty,
> Tyranny and atheism flowing through the realm...
>
> (III.ii.474–81)

Near the end of the play, before Montsurry's gang of hired murderers bursts in, the directions state: *Enter Monsieur and Guise above.* They place themselves in the gallery above the stage, watching in silence while their vengeance is enacted. For this stroke of dramatic technique Chapman may have been indebted to Kyd's *The Spanish Tragedy*, where the Ghost and Fury occupy a similar position as spectators of the tragedy that works itself out on stage.[13] But there is a significant difference. Chapman's Guise and Monsieur are human beings and historical figures, living representatives of the despotic state. Below, they watch the futile attempts of the Friar's ghost to protect Bussy. He succeeds for a moment, when the murderers, all but one, struck with fear of the supernatural, run back on hearing his voice. But the ghost has no un-earthly power; all he can rely on is vestigial superstition. Montsurry rallies his gang, taunting them for their cowardice, and leads them back. After that, all Bussy has to rely on is his personal valour. He fights mag-nificently, beating Montsurry to the ground, so confident that fate is on his side that he disdains to kill him. At this moment shots are fired at Bussy from off-stage; he falls mortally wounded, execrating 'the coward fates'. Actually the fates are on neither one side nor the other. Like the other abstractions of the play, nature, virtue, honour, fortune, they are only mental constructs. Bussy is killed by gunpowder, the first weapon of the modern state, which strikes out of reach of his sword, and is indifferent to human valour. Yet the concept is not altogether meaningless. Like nature, virtue and the rest, it projects the tragedy on a universal plane. In the last lines of the acting version of the play, the Friar's Ghost speaks Bussy's epitaph in words which identify him with Hercules, the mythical champion of mankind, defeated by the gods but transformed into a star that sets the universe ablaze with the fire of the human spirit.

> Farewell, brave relics of a complete man,
> Look up and see thy spirit made a star;
> Join flames with Hercules, and when thou sett'st
> Thy radiant forehead in the firmament
> Make the vast crystal crack with thy receipt;
> Spread to a world of fire, and the aged sky
> Cheer with new sparks of old humanity. (V.iv.147–53)

The Revenge of Bussy was written in 1610 or 1611, some years after *Bussy D'Ambois*, as a sequel to the revival of that play at the White-friars private theatre. Travis Bogard has said of it: 'There never was a work written for the professional stage that made fewer concessions to the audience.[14] One may remark that there never was in England an audience that expected fewer concessions to be made. The spectators at the private theatre in James I's reign consisted largely of young noblemen, university graduates, inns of court intellectuals and professional men. They, their relatives and friends were familiar with the centres of power; they understood its workings; and they made up a politically sophisticated, intellectually curious audience able to respond like few others to the complexities of the drama that Chapman provided.

Like *Bussy D'Ambois*, *The Revenge of Bussy* took as its subject the tragedy of an individual caught in the toils of state. But this time two themes were interrelated, appealing at different levels. The main action was dominated by an intellectual hero, a man of ideas, an exponent of principles. Clermont, the fictitious brother of the historical Bussy, expressed the opposite end of the Senecan polarity: the rationalist who was the alternative and complement to the rebellious titan. As a moral philosopher, as a Stoic, he cherished his immunity to the confused emotional urges that shaped the lives of lesser men. Against Clermont

[47]

were ranged, not jealous or dastardly men of state, but an apparatus of functionaries operating according to the impersonal processes of rule; immune, like himself, to enmity or affection. As counterpoint to this action, which, in keeping with the hero's character, moved on an intellectual plane, Chapman added a secondary action of private revenge, instigated by others, in which Clermont, against his nature and principles, was inescapably involved. The play thus combined two tragic modes. As heroic drama it was concerned with moral and political attitudes; as a revenge action it presented the passionate impulses of individuals. Each mode had its inherent limitations, and neither was planned to engage the unqualified sympathy of the audience. An unusual degree of critical detachment was called for. In the finale, however, a subtle dialectic brought into being a transformed response. This was neither total detachment nor total identification, but a pervading awareness of the tragic issue underlying the whole drama. It was not the assertion of ideas or doctrines; still less an enactment of the primitive justice of revenge; but a clarification of the ultimate, transcendent worth of human relationships.

As a sequel, *The Revenge of Bussy* recalls the characters and situations of the earlier play. In historical fact the murder of Bussy had led to a family quarrel that was peacefully composed by order of the King. But in Chapman's fiction it called forth a revenge action against Montsurry, instigated by Charlotte, the sister of Bussy, connived at by Tamyra, and drawing in the reluctant Clermont. Since, however, no further mention is made of Monsieur and the Guise as the true instigators of the murder, the revenge is without political significance. Unlike the revenge tragedies of Marston and Tourneur, it amounts to no more than a private feud, and its participants are, in keeping with the minor action, reduced to mere creatures of passion. Tamyra is no more than a shadow of her former self; Charlotte exists only for the enactment of vengeance. Montsurry appears as a passive, craven figure whose one object is to save his own skin. In contrast, the conflict between Clermont and the forces of state forms the major dynamic of the play. Here too the structure of the sequel required a return of the characters who in *Bussy* had embodied the workings of policy. The Guise and Monsieur accordingly reappear, but now in changed or subsidiary roles. Guise no longer represents the violence and corruption of the court. He is shown as the leader of a faction aiming at reform. Instead of opposing Clermont, he acts as his friend and patron, and professes to admire his high principles. The reforms Guise seeks are never specified, and his sincerity is an open question; but at least he is placed in a new relationship. As for Monsieur, he remains the cynic he had always been, and he features in one verbal duel with Clermont which calls to mind his old encounters with Bussy. But the dispute does not affect the action, and serves mainly to underline the difference between Bussy's impulsive response to provocation and his brother's careful, though far from cowardly restraint. Thereafter Monsieur disappears from the play, and is later reported to have died. The real antagonists to Clermont are neither Monsieur nor the Guise, but a hierarchy of officials from the King downwards.

In his political dramas up to *The Revenge of Bussy*, Chapman had avoided implicating the king himself in his denunciations of the workings of state. Henri III in *Bussy* took no part in the intrigues of his court politicians. His role had been mainly that of a choric commentator, even to the point of describing a world of natural 'noblesse' in which kings had no place. In the *Byron* plays Henri IV was presented as a well-deserving ruler whose achievements were a valid reply to Byron's seditious charges. Perhaps Chapman had wished to avoid more trouble with the authorities, who might construe attacks upon his French kings as covert criticisms of James I. But in *The Revenge*, whatever the reason, he abandoned this caution. Henri III reappears as an uneasy despot, operating an inhuman machinery of power through a chain of secret agents. Baligny, his chief functionary, poses as one of the faction of malcontents, informs on their activities, and plans the stratagems that defeat them. On stage through most of the first two acts, he is seen discoursing with the old dissident Renel, with Guise and with Clermont, besides reporting back to his royal master. A political chameleon, he adopts the opinions of every person he meets and even helps him to formulate his views. With Renel he holds forth eloquently on the corruption of society and the wickedness of 'policy'; no sooner has Renel departed than he explains his duty to look into 'discontented humours 'gainst the state'. He argues with equal conviction for and against political absolutism. To the King he puts forward a doctrine of totalitarian rule ignoring all moral values in the interests of state – 'though all men's reasons, All law, all conscience, concludes it wrong' (II.i.43–4). The theory is justified by analogies between the King's decrees and God's amounting to an ironical perversion of traditional concepts of order. To Guise in the same scene he supports the doctrine of revolt against tyranny, citing the precedent of Brutus:

> Caesar began to tyrannize; and when virtue
> Nor the religion of the Gods could serve

> To curb the insolence of his proud laws,
> Brutus would be the God's just instrument.   (II.i.109–12)

For good measure he adds a quotation from Sophocles' *Antigone*, that a king's laws cannot be compared with the edicts of God. For all these intellectual gyrations, what is most notable about Baligny is that as a person he is completely colourless. The touchy pride of Monsieur, the angry outbursts of Guise, are foreign to his nature. Satisfied with his record as a competent agent, he proudly disclaims all human ties:

> Your highness knows
> I will be honest, and betray for you
> Brother and father: for I know, my lord,
> Treachery for kings is truest loyalty
> Nor is to bear the name of treachery
> But grave, deep policy.   (II.i.29–34)

Not that Baligny is without regard for his self-advancement. Like all good stool-pigeons, he flatters his superiors, and knows that the more innocent the persons are whom he incriminates, the more credit accrues to himself for his zeal in trapping them. But this does not mark him out as an individual villain. His quest for victims is a normal part of the workings of a state system which depends on the zeal of its secret police. It is in the course of his duties, and through no personal animosity, that Baligny plans for the capture of Clermont who is his brother-in-law, knowing well that Clermont's association with Guise is politically harmless but confident that the arrest will enhance his own reputation.

Accordingly Clermont, like Bussy, becomes a target for the machinations of state. By secret arrangement with the King, he is invited to Baligny's country house during the tactful absence of its owner, is set upon while inspecting troops by soldiers suitably disguised as lackeys, and after a valiant struggle overpowered. Like Bussy in his turn, he is forewarned of the plot against him, but acts at first with characteristic caution. When Maillard, who is Baligny's agent in charge of the operation, comes to lead him into ambush he questions him closely and means to search him. He desists when Maillard swears by his faith to Clermont and to God that he means no harm. 'Who hath no faith to man, to God hath none', Maillard solemnly affirms, capping the celebrated adage of Montaigne.[15] After being at last captured by Chalon, the agent of Baligny's agent, Clermont recalls the oath, only to be told coolly that no perjury has been committed. 'You are no politician', Maillard replies:

                    not a fault
How foul soever, done for private ends,
Is fault in us, sworn to the public good.   (IV.i.48–50)

Betrayed down the chain of faceless agents, Clermont is indeed no
politician. Nevertheless he would probably have escaped their atten-
tions had he not involved himself in the world of politics. It is usually
thought that in Clermont Chapman portrayed his ideal hero, the 'Senecal man' of perfect integrity;[16] from which it is inferred that the
characterization is a failure, since Clermont's virtue seems priggish and
his moralizing pedantic. This is surely to underestimate Chapman's
artistry. There is no need to suppose that Clermont as he appears
through most of the play is meant to receive our unqualified admiration.
His limitations are all too plain. Assured that the society in which he
moves can be transformed by sweet reason, he is ready at the drop of a
hat to improvise scholarly lectures on Stoic morality. He cultivates
Guise, a hardened politician, in the belief that he will groom him for the
part of a philosopher-statesman. Our first encounter with Clermont,
engaged in a mimed conversation with Guise, is distanced by the
sardonic comments of Epernon and Monsieur:

EPERNON: He's now whispering in
          Some doctrine of stability and freedom,
          Contempt of outward greatness, and the guises[17]
          That vulgar great ones make their pride and zeal,
          Being only servile trains, and sumptuous houses,
          High places, offices.

MONSIEUR: Contempt of these
          Does he read to the Guise ? 'Tis passing needful.
          And he, I think, makes show t'affect his doctrine,
EPERNON: Commends, admires it –

MONSIEUR: And pursues another.   (I.i.153–61)

Like other politicians before him and since, the Guise finds it expedient
to patronize intellectuals and surround himself with a brains trust while
aspiring to office. Clermont takes his function very seriously, and in
return supports his patron's cause by justifying the unjustifiable. Baligny
in his pose as a malcontent has given fulsome praise to the Guise, but
even he had stopped short of approving Guise's part in the massacre of
Saint Bartholomew's day. Clermont, in contrast, imperturbably defends
it. The Protestants, he declares, were entirely to blame for their own
deaths. Did they not uphold the wrong faith and the wrong religion?

[51]

Did this not mean that they forfeited their rights to be considered as human beings ? In such cases, he affirms, 'Slain bodies are no more than oxen slain' (II.i.219). No English audience could possibly approve such theorizing in defence of mass slaughter. Clermont's readiness to over-look humanity in the furtherance of doctrine extends from politics to other fields. He has a mistress who literally weeps herself blind when he is captured. Yet he describes sexual love as a contradiction in terms. Sex, he maintains, is only an appetite: flies drink milk, bees collect honey; but they do not 'love' milk or honey; similarly it is absurd to talk of a man loving a woman (V.i.169–75).[18] After Chapman's revela-tion of the dark wisdom of love in the romance of Bussy and Tamyra, one can hardly suppose that this cold sophistry was meant to win sympathy. 'My brother speaks all principle', observes Charlotte after one of Clermont's discourses on the pursuit of good for its own sake. Even his Stoic indifference to his own fate, his conception of a man's duty 'To join himself with th'Universe In his main sway' rather than 'Wishing the complete Universe might be Subject to such a rag of it as he' is open to question as a statement of the play's primary values. The speech, based on Epictetus, is finely phrased, but it implies a contempt for the individual's place in the total scheme of things which, for all its seeming loftiness, is not far different in essence from the totalitarianism of Baligny.

Having been captured, Clermont is unexpectedly released from captivity, again by the King's order. This is not because Henri is con-cerned to do him justice, but because he is interested in bigger game and deems it expedient to accept Guise's defence of his protégé, while scheming to dispose of the Guise himself. Chapman wisely chose not to repeat the tragic finale of *Bussy* and show Clermont put to death by the machinations of state. The operation for his capture had suitably dramatized the workings of policy, but Clermont himself was at this point quite unqualified for the part of a tragic hero. Brave, no doubt, sincere enough in his convictions as a Stoic theoretician, Clermont was plainly deficient as a man. Mere expressions of high principles did not put him on a footing with the many-sided Bussy as a champion of man's aspirations to freedom. Here indeed lay the justification for the play's double action, which counterpointed the intellectualism of the main theme with the emotionalism of the revenge plot.

Hitherto, despite Tamyra's hatred of her husband and Charlotte's burning desire for vengeance, Clermont had shown a strong distaste for the ethics of the blood-feud. Only with full observance of chivalrous protocol, including the offer and acceptance of a formal challenge, had he been prepared to settle accounts with Montsurry. In the second act Montsurry had resorted to every dodge to avoid receiving the challenge, and the intended duel had been postponed. Now, with Clermont's release, new forces impel him to undertake the long-delayed revenge. In keeping with the Senecan tradition, Chapman introduces the ghost of Bussy, who rises and calls on his brother to take action. Suiting his elemental demand for blood to Clermont's need for intellectual conviction, the ghost delivers a reasoned discourse on the ethic of punishment. Since the state will not enact the justice for which it exists, the duty, says the ghost, devolves upon Clermont in person:

> What corrupted law
> Leaves unperformed in kings, do thou supply,
> And be above them all in dignity.   (V.i.97–9)

Clermont is persuaded, and in the last scene of the play enters upon the contest. As before, Montsurry's timorous evasions, his attempts to escape, his refusal to fight by lying on the floor, delay the formal duel and introduce a touch of comic relief. But at last even he rallies and rediscovers his manhood. The duel when it comes is fought out courageously, Montsurry offering Christian forgiveness to his opponent before his defeat. The death of Montsurry is followed by a spectacular effect: a grotesque rallying of the ghosts of Bussy, the Guise, Monsieur, and even characters not appearing in the drama, who perform a dance of triumph round the victim's body.

T. M. Parrott, the editor of Chapman's dramas, commented on this dance of the ghosts, seeing it as 'an attempt on the part of the management of the Whitefriars Theatre to add a little spectacular divertissement'.[19] But the grotesquery is fully in keeping with Chapman's whole treatment of the revenge tradition in this play. The lengthy philosophizing of the ghost of Bussy, who is seen only by Clermont and not by Guise, though he is present, the antics of Montsurry in avoiding the duel, the bizarre masque of irrelevant ghosts after Montsurry's death, contain an element of parody which serves to isolate the revenge theme and make it evident to the audience that sympathetic identification is not called for. Instead, a more complex dramatic effect is obtained. Chapman suggests the partial and inadequate nature of the attitudes to life presented so far on *both* levels of his play. The revenge emotions of the minor theme, distanced by the tone of parody, offset the ideality of the main theme, which had likewise been treated with a degree of critical reserve. Neither mere passion nor mere intellectuality sufficed to make Clermont a tragic hero. But in a final dénouement, intellect and passion were fused together on a different plane from that on which either had been presented, and Clermont at last stood forth not as the abstract Senecal man, nor as a conventional revenge hero, but as a complete and suffering human being.

It is on the supremacy of human values that the play at last comes to rest. Unlike the revenge tragedies of Shakespeare, Marston, and Tourneur, the avenging of Bussy leaves the state order intact. Nor is the action against Clermont directed at a hero of sufficient stature to present a challenge to the corrupt political world. What finally destroys Clermont is an act which transforms his personality from within. A few moments after his victory over Montsurry he learns that the king has killed Guise; and with this comes the realization that without his friend life has no further meaning. Chapman's tragic resolution is too abruptly arrived at and insufficiently prepared; but its significance should not be overlooked. The play allowed extraordinary scope for the elaboration of ideas. The facts and causes of social decline, the arguments for and against absolutism, the Stoic attitudes towards ambition, honour, and man's place in the universe were set forth with much eloquence. But ultimately these abstract questions are all made to subserve one essential issue, the relationship of man to man. Maillard's forsworn declaration to Clermont, 'Who hath no faith to men, to God hath none', becomes in positive form the principle upon which human existence depends. The repudiation of this in the interests of state invalidates the political world more completely than any concept or theory.[20] Throughout the play Clermont had viewed himself as the exponent of right ideas, the propounder of noble attitudes. Doctrine had depleted his humanity. With the murder of the Guise at the King's orders he discovers that his true motivation was neither political idealism nor philosophical truth, but the primordial loyalty of man to man. The state in destroying this foundation has drained life of its meaning. Survival in a dehumanized society is no more than slavery. Clermont resolves not to remain exposed to 'all the horrors of the vicious time'. Before his suicide he sees himself, in a fine extended simile, as a mariner left exposed on the dangerous shores of a savage land, when his captain the Guise has already sailed for the open sea:

> Now, then, as a ship,
> Touching at strange and far-removed shores,
> Her men ashore go, for their several ends,

Fresh water, victuals, precious stones, and pearl,
All yet intentive (when the master calls,
The ship to put off ready) to leave all
Their greediest labours, lest they there be left
To thieves or beasts, or be the country's slaves:
So, now my master calls, my ship, my venture,
All in one bottom cast, all quite put off,
Gone under sail; and I left negligent,
To all the horrors of the vicious time,
The far-remov'd shores to all virtuous aims,
None favouring goodness, none but he respecting
Piety nor manhood – shall I here survive,
Not cast me after him into the sea,
Rather than here live, ready every hour
To feed thieves, beasts, and be the slave of power?
I come, my lord! Clermont, thy creature, comes.   (V.v.175–93)

The sea, with its vast expanses, its unknown perils, provides the opening image of *Bussy D'Ambois* and the last image of its sequel. It seems to me – this is only a personal impression – that Clermont's last speech was suggested to Chapman by some episode of the *Odyssey*. If so, it serves to intimate a striking contrast between Clermont and Odysseus. Clermont, who had patterned his life upon an ideal of wisdom and self-sufficiency, likens himself at death not to the great Homeric captain, but to a humble sailor left behind in a savage land, in danger of becoming 'the slave of power'. His only saviour is the friend who, like the friend of Shakespeare's sonnets, is the object of an entirely selfless devotion. Clermont's new-found humility adds to his dramatic stature. In giving up his lofty pretensions, he meets his end as an authentic tragic hero.

NOTES

1. *Chapman's Homer*, ed. Allardyce Nicoll (1957), Vol. II, p. 5.
2. Ennis Rees, *The Tragedies of George Chapman: Renaissance Ethics in Action* (1954), p. 30.
3. Rees thought that Chapman in this passage 'drew weighty moral significance from the wrath of Achilles ... to leave no doubt as to whether or not they [Bussy and Byron] were to be regarded as examples of evil'; in contrast, Chapman's 'ethical sympathy' lay with such 'virtuous heroes' as Clermont (p. 31). Chapman does not in fact refer explicitly to either Achilles or Odysseus; he describes, quite objectively, two kinds of 'virtue',

a term whose Renaissance connotations were broader than the restricted moral sense. If the passage is to be applied to the plays, both Bussy and Clermont qualify as 'virtuous heroes'. (See Robert J. Lordi, Introduction to *Bussy D'Ambois*, Regents Renaissance Drama Series (1964), pp. xxiv-xxvi, and Waith, *The Herculean Hero*, pp. 16-17.)

4. Waith, p. 34, notes the ambivalence in Seneca between quietism and aspiration, and points out the obtrusion in a passage praising *mediocria* (*Moral Epistles* XXXIX) of the comment: 'No man of exalted gifts is pleased with what is low and mean; the vision of great achievement summons him and uplifts him. Just as the flame springs straight into the air and cannot be cabined or kept down, any more than it can repose in quiet, so our soul is always in motion, and the more ardent it is, the greater its motion and activity.' (Translated Richard M. Gummere.)

5. See Roy W. Battenhouse, *Marlowe's Tamburlaine: A Study in Renaissance Moral Philosophy* (1941); Douglas Cole, *Suffering and Evil in the Plays of Christopher Marlowe* (1962); Franklin M. Dickey, *Not Wisely But Too Well: Shakespeare's Love Tragedies* (1957). A balanced account of recent critical attitudes to Marlowe is presented by Irving Ribner in 'Marlowe and the Critics', *Tulane Drama Review* VIII (1964), pp. 211-14.

6. Ennis Rees, p. 28.

7. Irving Ribner, *Jacobean Tragedy: The Quest for Moral Order* (1962), pp. 23-5. Ribner rejects the simplistic view of *Bussy D'Ambois* as a 'cautionary example' and insists that the play be considered as a tragedy. But the tragedy functions, in his view, strictly within the framework of Christian doctrine. It is occasioned by 'the fall of man from Paradise and the consequent corruption of nature', necessitating order and degree, institutions and laws. Bussy is 'a symbol of prelapsarian perfection', as well as a type of the common man, entering the world of corruption and inevitably tainted by it. Without being crudely didactic, this interpretation may still be thought to accommodate *Bussy* to the morality play tradition rather than accept it as a Renaissance secular drama.

8. Robert Ornstein, *The Moral Vision of Jacobean Tragedy*, pp. 57-9. 'Intended as an anti-Prince, Bussy eventually becomes a Stoic version of the Prince, who must transcend conventional law to reform his society.'

9. Alice Shalvi, Introduction to Bertrand de Loque, *Discourses of Warre and Single Combat* (1591), Renaissance Library Facsimile Edition (1968), p. viii.

10. I have accepted and extended G. R. Hibbard's comparison: 'Indeed, is it going too far to say that Bussy putting the case for "man in his native noblesse" is . . . not so far removed from figures like John Lilburne?' ('Chapman: Tragedy and the Providential View of History', *Shakespeare Survey* 20 (1967), p. 30.)

11. Ornstein sees the Friar as 'a politic bawd . . . who views lust as an appetite that must be satisfied' (p. 56). Yet there is a world of difference between Chapman's Friar and such court bawds as Shakespeare's Pandarus. He is, in the dramatic and poetical context, rather the priest of nature, ministering to man's natural virtues. The contrast is similarly present in Marston's *The Dutch Courtesan*, where Malheureux envies the mating of the 'freeborn birds':

> They have no bawds, no mercenary beds,
> No politic restraints, no artificial heats,
> No faint dissembling; no custom makes them blush,
> No shame afflicts their name. O you happy beasts,
> In whom an inborn heat is not held sin,
> How far transcend you wretched, wretched man,
> Whom national customs, tyrannous respects
> Of slavish order, fetters, lames his power,
> Calling that sin in us which in all things else
> Is Nature's highest virtue!   (II.i.69–78)

Marston finally brings the scales down on the side of conventional against natural morality; but the daring and eloquence of this speech makes it stand in its own right.

12. Waith, *The Herculean Hero*, p. 98. Peter Bement in 'The Imagery of Darkness and Light in Chapman's *Bussy D Ambois*', *Studies in Philology* LXIV (1967), pp. 187–98, sees Chapman's conception of Night as related to 'a mystical Neoplatonic tradition' which dissociated darkness from evil. Bement is nevertheless perturbed by the neglect of 'moral virtues' as the play unfolds; he finds it necessary to dismiss Tamyra's invocation as 'irony', and to claim that the night of the play after Act I is not the true one, but the 'stepdame Night of minde' mentioned in Chapman's *Hymnus in Noctem*, lines 63 ff. – Whatever Chapman meant by the 'night of mind', or intellectual darkness, this phrase has surely no bearing on the impassioned experience of Bussy and Tamyra, or the magic of Behemoth. Night is associated with love, 'naked virtues', 'longings' and 'joy' in the Epithalamion of Chapman's Fifth Sestiad to *Hero and Leander*. Even more in keeping with the experience of the play are the closing lines of *Hymnus in Noctem*, celebrating the orgiastic advent of night:

> See now ascends, the glorious Bride of Brides,
> Nuptials, and triumphs, glittring by her sides . . .
> Behind her, with a brase of siluer Hynds,
> In Iuorie chariot, swifter then the winds,
> Is great Hyperions horned daughter drawne
> Enchantresse-like, deckt in disparent lawne,
> Circkled with charmes, and incantations,
> That ride huge spirits, and outragious passions.

(*The Poems of George Chapman*, ed. Phyllis Brooks Bartlett (1941, 1962) *Hymnus in Noctem*, lines 384–5, 392–7.)

13. 'The grim presences sit above, and for them the audience in the court of Spain is composed of actors in a larger, predestined drama.' Anne Righter, *Shakespeare and the Idea of the Play* (1962), p. 81. The assumption that in Kyd's play the Ghost and Andrea sit in the gallery above stage has recently been questioned (Barry B. Adams, 'The Audiences of *The Spanish Tragedy*', *Journal of English and Germanic Philology* LXVIII (1969), p. 225). Chapman's own stage direction is clear, and the close resemblance between his dramatic effect and Kyd's strongly suggests the use of the gallery at least in revived performances of *The Spanish Tragedy*.

14. Travis Bogard, *The Tragic Satire of John Webster* (1955), p. 33.

15. 'I answered not long since, that hardly could I betray my Prince for a particular man, who should be very sorry to betray a particular man for my Prince.' Montaigne, *Essays*, translated Florio, III.1 (Everyman edition Vol. 3, pp. 8–9).

16. Cf. Parrott: 'Chapman's full-length portrait of the perfect man of Stoic doctrine placed in a Renaissance setting . . . an ideal of character and conduct that, regarded from the ethical point of view, is stronger and loftier than any to be found in contemporary drama.' *The Plays of George Chapman*, ed. T. M. Parrott: *The Tragedies* (1910, 1961), Vol. II, p. 575.

17. The pun on 'Guise' and 'guises' would have been obvious in the pronunciation of Chapman's time.

18. Chapman's own attitude may be gauged from the far subtler use of the image in a non-dramatic context. In his addition to *Hero and Leander* the bees, though pursuing their own ends, prepare the way for the wax to perform its 'proper virtue'; so the sexual instinct leads to the human fulfilment of love:

> When Bees makes waxe, Nature doth not intend
> It shall be made a Torch: but we that know
> The proper virtue of it make it so,
> And when 'tis made we light it: nor did Nature
> Propose one life to maids, but each such creature
> Makes by her soule the best of her free state,
> Which without loue is rude, disconsolate,
> And wants loues fire to make it milde and bright,
> Till when, maids are but Torches wanting light.
>
> (Sixth Sestiad, lines 67–75)

19. Parrott, II. p. 587 (note to *The Revenge of Bussy*, V.v.119).

20. 'The ultimate horror of policy, Chapman suggests, is not its rationalization of inhuman acts but its destruction of the fundamental trust upon which society rests' (Ornstein, p. 71).

IV

Roman Tragedy:
Sejanus, Caesar and Pompey

In an article entitled 'Shakespeare on the Modern Stage: Past Significance and Present Meaning',[1] Robert Weimann takes up the question
of how a modern producer should interpret Shakespeare's plays. A
purely academic approach seeking to restore the original conditions
at the Globe is ruled out, if only because one can never restore the most
important element, the audience itself. However 'Elizabethan' the
performance, the original *rapport* between characters and spectators
cannot be brought back. On the other hand, nothing is truly gained by
fashionable attempts to force the plays into a contemporary mould,
making Hamlet, say, an angry young man, Brutus an existentialist, and
so on. A producer should rather accept the necessary tension between
present and past and bring out the historical continuity between them.
'We are all characters in history,' Weimann remarks; 'our own points
of reference are, like Shakespeare's, products of history. In this, our
present values emerge from the same historical process which is both
reflected in, and accelerated by, Shakespeare's contribution.'[2]

This awareness of identity in change, so needful for an understanding
of the past, was very much in the minds of Shakespeare's generation.
Through the Italy of the revenge plays, Marston and others related the
issues of their time to the most blatant examples of tyranny and revolt
in Europe. In recent French history Chapman found a mirror for the
more sophisticated form of state absolutism in his own land. But neither
the Italy of petty despots nor the centralized monarchy of France
offered the range and clarity of perspective to be found in Roman
history. Here, set forth with objectivity and a careful marshalling of
facts, was the story of the rise and fall of a world republic; the rivalries
of dictators; the overthrow of free institutions, and their replacement
by a despotism based on demagogy, a system of informers, and a universal debasement of values. Plutarch's *Lives*, translated by North,
provided a whole gallery of vivid portraits of the men engaged in these
struggles, making Cato, Pompey, Brutus, Julius Caesar and Antony

virtual contemporaries. Tacitus in his *Annals* described with calm objectivity the intrigues and manoeuvres of Imperial Rome. Sallust in *The Catiline War* wrote the epitaph on a civilization whose resemblance to that of the Renaissance could hardly be missed:

> Those who had found it easy to bear hardship and dangers, anxiety and adversity, found leisure and wealth . . . a burden and a curse. Hence the lust for power first, then for money, grew upon them; these were . . . the root of all evils. For avarice destroyed honour, integrity, and all other noble qualities; taught in their place insolence, cruelty, to neglect the gods, to set a price on everything . . . At first these vices grew slowly; from time to time they were punished; finally, when the disease had spread like a deadly plague, the state was changed and a government second to none in equity and excellence became cruel and intolerable.[3]

Influenced by these writers, the dramatists of a new age of despotism and predatory commerce were quick to realize that ancient history provided a sounding-board for the conflicts in which their own society was engaged. Renaissance literary theory supported them in declaring that the subject-matter for tragedy in their age was neither mythology nor everyday life but historical events. A proper approach, it was added, required not the mere repetition of facts, but a selective treatment which concentrated on the features of history which had permanent relevance. The dramatists of the age found these in the workings of power, the concept of freedom, and the bearings of history itself upon the fortunes of the individual.[4] More specifically, they recognized as the period of maximum tension the years which marked the rise of Caesar and the civil wars leading to the replacement of the republic by the empire.

Most of us today think of Roman tragedy exclusively in terms of Shakespeare's plays. We have even learned our ancient history through Shakespeare and form our mental pictures of Caesar, Brutus, Cassius, and Mark Antony from his characters. Without contesting the dramatic force which has produced this effect, it is well to bear in mind that Shakespeare's was only one expression of a great current of ideas and attitudes. Something may be gained by seeing the Roman plays of other Jacobean dramatists not as inferior versions of Shakespeare's but as direct successors to a European tradition. The creators of this tradition, such writers as Cinthio and Pescetti in Italy, Jodelle and Garnier in France, Daniel and Alexander in England, based their dramas on their readings of classical history and drew their characters, as Shakespeare did, from Plutarch. But they were less preoccupied than Shakespeare with character as such, and more concerned with the political forces actuating individuals. In the glass of history they saw the movements of their own time distanced and given a permanent validity. It is worth emphasizing that their conception of these movements was very different from the medieval attitudes taken up into the Tudor myth of absolutism, so often seen as the major influence on writers of the age. It is true that in medieval times Julius Caesar was regarded as a legendary hero, one of the Nine Worthies, a miscellaneous group which included Joshua, Judas Maccabeus, Charlemagne and King Arthur; while Brutus and Cassius were seen as scoundrelly regicides. But the dramatists who knew their Plutarch recognized in Caesar the prime factor in the destruction of the Roman Commonwealth, the prototypal dictator with whose modern successors they were all too well acquainted. We have been told that in the sixteenth century republicanism was little understood; that absolute monarchy was the order of the day; that the busts of the Twelve Emperors adorned palaces all over Europe.[5] Certainly they did; but one would hardly expect to find statues of Brutus in the palaces of Renaissance princes, any more than to see portraits of Lenin in the Pentagon. The fact is that Brutus, the killer of Caesar, and his ancestor who founded the Roman republic, were very much in the thoughts of sixteenth-century Europeans. In France the anonymous classic of political radicalism, *Vindiciae Contra Tyrannos*, 'Vengeance Against Tyrants', appeared in 1579 under the pseudonym 'Junius Brutus'. Translated from Latin into French, from French into English, reprinted eight times in the seventeenth century in England alone, including such crucial dates as 1648 and 1689, it inspired democratic thinkers for two centuries. Tyrants were described therein as 'like the viperous brood which gnaws through the entrails of their own mother: as be those generals of armies created by the people, who afterwards, by the means of those forces, make themselves masters of the state, as Caesar at home under the pretence of the dictatorship, and divers princes of Italy'.[6] Italy had indeed seen political liberty stamped out in state after state by the installation of foreign rulers and their puppets. The Republic of Florence, home of free institutions for centuries, had been overthrown in 1530 after three years of siege and attrition. If absolutism had become the order of the day, few Italians could regard it as a blessed or even necessary event. Nor was tyrannicide popularly regarded as a crime, but rather as an honourable tradition kept alive by the memory of such martyrs as Olgiato.[7]

These attitudes find dramatic expression in Pescetti's tragedy *Il Cesare*, published in 1594, which treats Brutus and Cassius with the sympathy shown by Shakespeare only a few years later. The two plays have noticeable resemblances in outlook and treatment. Both take their material from Plutarch's *Lives*. Both give important parts to Portia and Calpurnia, making the personal, feminine element temper some of the grimness of the central action. There are nevertheless some outstanding differences. Pescetti shows a more overt commitment to the ideals of the conspirators. In his play Brutus has no inner doubts as to the justice of killing Caesar. Nor is Cassius shown as motivated by personal jealousy. Brutus is introduced in Act I, walking alone, deep in meditation. Cassius encounters him and asks what has made him leave his bed at this early hour. Grief at Rome's suffering, Brutus replies; he can no longer restrain his urge to free the city. Cassius rejoices at what he has heard:

> In this way, Brutus, we ascend to heaven,
> By killing tyrants, rescuing the oppressed,
> Purging the world of cruel monsters.   (I.196–8)[8]

In this version, we notice, the initiative for the conspiracy comes from Brutus; Cassius only seconds him. The next to enter is Portia, anxious, like Shakespeare's Portia, to know what is troubling her husband. She makes an impetuous plea to be taken into the confidence of the two men:

> Now, by the love you bear our dead Republic,
> Faithful companions, I conjure you, on whom
> Alone rests what small hope remains for our
> Declining Roman state, that you unveil
> Your thoughts.   (II.351–5)

They tell her their secret, and she begs to join them and take part in the assassination of Caesar. Though finally persuaded to remain at home, she speeds them on their way:

> Go forth, ye strong and wise. Go forth, ye are
> Worthy of your high lineage. May heaven
> Second your wishes.   (II.387–9)

Less concerned with personal affections than Shakespeare's Portia, Pescetti's counterpart voices with passionate directness the secret aspirations of Renaissance Italy. Tragedy lies in the recognition that they are doomed to failure. A similar note is struck in the Cleopatra plays of Cinthio, of Jodelle and Garnier in France and Daniel in England. Following the Senecan tradition, they observe unity of time and place, and commence their action near the end of the train of events, after Antony's defeat at the battle of Actium, which in Shakespeare's *Antony and Cleopatra* is not reached until Act IV. The story is thus confined to Octavius Caesar's attempt to carry away Cleopatra as a captive to Rome, Cleopatra's ruses to outwit him by a show of submission, and her suicide, 'in order', as she declares, 'to escape Servitude and deep shame'.⁹ The central theme of the tragedy lies in the resolve of the defeated queen to die rather than fall into the hands of a foreign conqueror. Other aspects of Cleopatra's life and love which might distract us from this major issue are omitted or glossed over. There is nothing of Shakespeare's magnificent courtesan about these treatments of the heroine and certainly no attempt to draw a pious moral making Cleopatra's fall a cautionary example of the results of sinful desire. She regards herself as Antony's *de facto* wife and is entirely devoted to the memory of her great consort. Besides this, she is depicted as the loving mother of children whom Octavius has ousted from the throne of their native land. In all her actions Cleopatra is made to seem, as Daniel calls her,

> The wonder of her kinde, of rarest spirit,
> A glorious Lady, and a mighty Queene.
> *The Tragedie of Cleopatra*, 1599   (1360–61)

Jonson's Roman tragedy *Sejanus* stems from this tradition. Like the writers just mentioned, he was more concerned with the political forces at work in history than with virtuous or vicious individuals. Like these writers, he based his drama on recorded facts, not legend or myth. But there are distinctive features about his approach. An unparalleled thoroughness of scholarship went into his preparations. He took his material mainly from Tacitus, the most objective of classical historians, supplementing this with abundant details from other writers. But Jonson was concerned with more than mere factual accuracy. If his careful listing of sources in the margin of the text gives an impression of pedantry, a reading of the play itself shows a careful shaping of his material to bring out the main issues and their contemporary relevance. Jonson's artistic energies were fully at work, imposing a form and pattern on history, making it reflect, without any violation of the truth, his own sombre vision of life. In the process he drew upon the experience he had gained over years of experimentation with comic satire. In the plays between *Every Man In His Humour* in 1598 and *Sejanus* in 1603, Jonson had deliberately broken away from the Elizabethan mode of sympathetic characterization and learnt to present human follies with icy detachment. Affectations and absurdities were not treated with gentle humour but exposed to harsh ridicule. Now, in his dramatization of history, comic satire on individuals gave way to satire on the plane of tragedy. Ridicule was replaced by a fierce yet controlled indignation, directed not at private folly but at the debasement of a civilization. In this treatment there was no room for idealism and pathos. *Sejanus* was a play without heroes or heroines, without rousing declamations or expressions of visionary hope. Audiences at the Globe missed the intimate engagement with character of Shakespeare's *Julius Caesar*, and to this day its grim severity works against popular stage presentation. Nevertheless this tragedy, which exposes the fatal flaw in history, the pity and terror of the world of state, is, like Shakespeare's, for all time.[10] Hazlitt, living in the post-Napoleonic period of repression, saw its significance in his own era, and in the present age of super-powers and super-demagogy Jonson's portrait of the state in its most monstrous, hypertrophied form is full of ominous correspondences.

Sejanus is set in the reign of Tiberius, eighty years after the great struggles of the civil war. The Roman republic has been irreversibly transformed into a world empire. What had once been a free society is now governed by a degenerate, ageing autocrat and his personally appointed favourite. Lip-service is still paid to the constitutional forms of the past, but the spirit of liberty has died out with the passing of its former champions.

> The men are not the same! 'Tis we are base,
> Poor and degenerate from th' exalted strain
> Of our great fathers. Where is now the soul
> Of God-like Cato ? – he that durst be good
> When Caesar durst be evil, and had power
> As not to live his slave, but die his master ?
> Or where the constant Brutus, that, being proof
> Against all charm of benefits, did strike
> So brave a blow into the monster's heart
> That sought unkindly to captive his country ? . . .
> Brave Cassius was the last of all that race.   (1.87–96, 104)

In the new dispensation, hypocrisy and terror have eroded human dignity. The senators vie with one another in acclaiming every utterance of Tiberius and flattering his upstart minister Sejanus. Potential opponents are spied on by a network of secret agents. To present the situation in its true light Jonson employed a form of alienation technique, setting a group of commentators on the stage whose criticism served to interpret and 'place' the duplicity of the regime. Dissidents who can only speak but not act, and are due themselves to be incriminated one by one, they expose to the audience the real motivations of Sejanus and Tiberius, beneath professions of patriotism and devotion to the public good. Like Vindice in *The Revenger's Tragedy*, who castigates the court as it passes across the stage, Jonson's commentators Arruntius, Silius, and Sabinus stand apart from the autocracy and its servants, providing a satirical chorus through most of the play. But Jonson's satire operates with a political sophistication unlike Tourneur. Tiberius, Sejanus and their hangers-on are seen as representative politicians in a degenerate state, not walking embodiments of vice. Arruntius and his group foster no ingenuous belief that Caesarian tyranny with its troops and secret police can be wiped out by a simple plot of revengers in disguise. History, not wishful thinking, shapes the action of the play, and tragic force is given to the satire by the absence of any hope in a happy ending.

Through a succession of brief appearances by the leading character, pointed up satirically by Arruntius and his friends, the political situation is made clear. Tiberius, a master of hypocrisy, is seen disclaiming the personality cult which is implicit in his position, publicly refusing divine honours while accepting in private the gross flattery of his court. Sejanus the favourite, professing limitless devotion to his imperial master, receives complete executive power, which he will employ to eliminate the heirs to Tiberius, with the ultimate aim of becoming emperor in his place. These heirs include Drusus, the emperor's son, an outspoken critic of Sejanus, and the offspring of Germanicus, Tiberius's popular brother. Before the action began, Germanicus, so named from his victorious campaigns against the German tribes, had been removed from the centre of political activities by the familiar device of an appointment abroad. As Sabinus says,

> When men grow so fast
> Honoured and loved, there is a trick in state
> Which jealous princes never fail to use ...
> Either by embassy, the war, or such,
> To shift them forth into another air
> Where they may purge, and lessen.   (I.159–61, 164–6)

Once out of sight in his diplomatic appointment, Germanicus was

[65]

exposed to provocations by secret agents; when he resisted their designs he was finally poisoned. Agrippina his widow and his three young sons survive, a rallying point for opponents of the regime, but powerless to act and subject to constant surveillance by imperial spies.

Step by step Sejanus's projects are advanced. His first victim is Drusus. Employing a bribed physician as his go-between, Sejanus seduces Livia, Drusus's wife, and all three devise a plot whereby Drusus is poisoned. Thereafter Sejanus works upon Tiberius's fears to persuade him that the family of Germanicus and their supporters constitute a serious danger. Plans are made for the opposition to be eliminated, not by a single spectacular stroke, but by the use of what we have learned to call 'salami tactics', a gradual technique for disposing of political enemies one by one. At a meeting of the Senate presided over by Tiberius, the sons of Germanicus receive fulsome praise while their supporters are accused of crimes against the state. Silius, a fearless old general, is charged with extortion and treason; Cordus, a distinguished historian, with slandering Tiberius in his works. Sabinus, a third member of the opposition, is trapped by secret agents. When the process is complete the children of Germanicus are banished or put under house arrest. Sejanus consolidates his position by encouraging the old emperor to retire to Capri and indulge his secret vices away from the public view. Meanwhile Sejanus stays in Rome, building up support amongst the troops stationed round the capital and concentrating all power in his own hands.

Without stage horrors or sensational effects, Jonson's play depicts with timeless relevance a society in the grip of state terror. Tiberius presides over the Senate with a show of judicial impartiality while his corrupt prosecutors make their trumped-up accusations. Cordus is charged with having published a history in which Brutus is praised and Cassius described as 'the last of all the Romans'. After an eloquent defence of the freedom of the pen, he is remanded, – but immediate orders are given for his books to be burnt. The commentators drive home the significance of such measures.

> Let 'em be burnt! Oh, how ridiculous
> Appears the Senate's brainless diligence
> Who think they can, with present power, extinguish
> The memory of all succeeding times!...
> Nor do they aught, that use this cruelty
> Of interdiction, and this rage of burning,

> But purchase to themselves rebuke and shame,
> And to the writers an eternal name.   (III.471–4, 477–80)[11]

Silius, likewise accused by nonentities, had already concluded a speech of intrepid defiance by stabbing himself:

> Romans, if any here be in this senate
> Would know to mock Tiberius' tyranny,
> Look upon Silius, and so learn to die.   (III.337–9)

Sabinus is spied on in his own house by two agents concealed in the rafters, while a third provokes him into an outburst against the imperial tyrant. He is seized and led away, to be dragged by a hook down the steps of the Gemonies and flung into the Tiber. Arruntius, the one surviving commentator, voices with savage irony the dread of all decent men living through times of state terror:

> May I pray to Jove
> In secret, and be safe? Aye, or aloud?
> With open wishes? So I do not mention
> Tiberius or Sejanus? Yes, I must
> If I speak out. 'Tis hard, that. May I think
> And not be rack'd? What danger is't to dream,
> Talk in one's sleep, or cough? Who knows the law?
> May I shake my head without a comment? Say
> It rains, or it holds up, and not be thrown
> Upon the Gemonies?   (IV.300–9)

The turning point comes when Sejanus, supremely confident of his influence over Tiberius, over-reaches himself by asking permission to marry Drusus' widow Livia, already his mistress. As soon as Sejanus has left, Tiberius appoints Macro as his personal agent to spy on the over-ambitious favourite and, when the time is ripe, to bring about his downfall. Macro is the perfect instrument of state. Like Chapman's Baligny he is utterly without scruples, and lets no private loyalty count against his zeal for promotion.

> Were it to plot against the fame, the life
> Of one with whom I twinned; remove a wife
> From my warm side, as loved as is the air;
> Practice away each parent: draw mine heir
> In compass, though but one; work all my kin
> To swift perdition; leave no untrained engine
> For friendship, or for innocence; nay, make

[67]

The gods all guilty: I would undertake
This, being imposed me, both with gain and ease.
The way to rise is to obey and please.   (III.726–35)

Macro accordingly goes about his secret task, investigating Sejanus's activities beneath a cloak of deference, and building up his own military guard. Tiberius for his part creates a smoke-screen by a series of confusing and contradictory messages. The day of reckoning arrives when the Senate is unexpectedly summoned to hear an epistle from the emperor. With Macro's guards stationed at the doors the message is read out. With supreme deviousness it shifts back and forth between praise and criticism of Sejanus, while the Senators strain to comprehend Tiberius's true drift. Finally the epistle recommends that Sejanus be stripped of his offices, suggests that the Senate might think fit to seize his property, and delicately hints that justice might require the forfeit of his life. Politic to the last, Tiberius dresses his *coup* in the trappings of legality. But no delicacy is required of Macro, who immediately assumes military command and without further ado has Sejanus hauled off to execution.

In appearance, Jonson's dramatic structure accords with medieval conceptions of tragedy as depicting the fall of the great at the turning of Fortune's wheel. But in essence it amounts to a denial of the moral principles underlying such concepts. Sejanus falls in one day from the height of power to the lowest degradation, his body torn to pieces by the mob so that the executioner cannot even do his work. But the story provides no elevating lesson. Unless the cunning voluptuary Tiberius is to be equated with God, divine providence has no part in the action. Even that equivocal deity Fortune, both invoked and defied by Sejanus in Act V, exercises no influence and may be dismissed as a mental construct. As Jonas A. Barish, the Yale editor of the play, remarks, 'the margin allowed to unseen or unknown or uncontrollable forces dwindles nearly to the vanishing point.'[12] History is made by men; it is as ruthless and amoral as they; and for Jonson it offers no hope of amelioration. The fall of Sejanus marks the rise of Macro, an equally unprincipled scoundrel whose first act is to order the murder of his victim's innocent children. His mental level may be gauged by his treatment of Sejanus's young daughter:

... because our laws
Admit no virgin immature to die,
The wittily and strangely cruel Macro

Deliver'd her to be deflower'd and spoiled
By the rude lust of the licentious hangman,
Then to be strangled with her harmless brother.   (V.849-54)

The people who, if Sejanus had succeeded in his designs, would have acclaimed him as emperor, savage him blindly when disgraced, 'And not a beast of all that herd demands What was his crime, or who were his accusers'. As for the tyranny of state, the police terror, the universal hypocrisy and corruption, these continue unabated. Jonson's devastating satire portrays not the tragedy of one man but of a whole society in the political inferno of its own creation.

In contrast to Jonson's monolithic achievement, Chapman's *Caesar and Pompey* suffers from a diversity of methods and artistic aims. Classical restraint, as in the use of set speeches, messengers' reports, and Senecan aphorisms, co-exists with the flamboyance of the Elizabethan history play, and the three middle acts are clamorous with battle-scenes, alarms, excursions and deaths on stage. Nor is this all. The play opens with a political debate conducted with the finesse of a skilled chess-game, in which every move involves an intricacy of monoeuvre only to be appreciated by those long familiar with public affairs. The latter scenes, moreover, introduce philosophical discourses on the ethics of suicide and the grounds for belief in an after-life which put a strain on the attention of any popular audience. Underlying these disparate techniques we may detect the variety of Chapman's concerns. As always, his interests were deeply engaged in the political world and the workings of state. But unlike Jonson, he was either unable or unwilling to subordinate all considerations to one overriding theme. He was equally preoccupied with the spectacle of great individuals shaping, and themselves shaped, by the processes of history, and with the ultimate question of human values in the face of a hostile world and an inscrutable universe. The result is a play which appeals on many levels but fails to make a unified impact. Critics more concerned with moral patterns than artistic processes abstract from *Caesar and Pompey* whatever doctrine or attitude they find most congenial. The play has been hailed as an apology for Christian humanism, regardless of the secular issues that provide most of the dramatic tension and the unresolved antinomies of its thought.[13] It has been described as 'a twilight study lost in the shadows of Aurelian meditation';[14] a beautiful phrase, perhaps, but oddly unsuited to a play whose action shades over from verbal polemic to battles to murder to a prolonged *hara-kiri* on stage. *Caesar and Pompey*, like all Chapman's dramas, is concerned with the

human predicament in all its paradoxes and contradictions, and sub-
serves no doctrine or intellectual thesis. If I consider it here chiefly in
its bearing on the Jacobean preoccupation with man in the world of
state, I shall nevertheless try to avoid reducing its complexities to a
formula.

As a history play, *Caesar and Pompey* turns back to the crucial period
of western civilization eighty years before the time of Jonson's *Sejanus*,
and dramatizes the conflict between the two great military rivals whose
outcome was the destruction of republican freedom and the establishment of a despotic world state. At the opening of the play Caesar's
army is poised waiting to invade Roman territory while the forces of
Pompey, the champion of the republic, prepare to oppose it. No doubt
is left in our minds as to the intentions of Caesar or the nature of his
proto-fascist supporters, the riff-raff of all Europe, avid for place and
rewards:

> Look how, against great rains, a standing pool
> Of paddocks, toads and water-snakes put up
> Their speckled throats above the venomous lake
> Croaking and gasping for some fresh fall'n drops . . .
> So still where Caesar goes there thrust up head
> Impostors, flatterers, favourites and bawds,
> Buffoons, intelligencers, select wits,
> Close murderers, mountebanks and decay'd thieves,
> To gain their baneful lives relief from him,
> From Britain, Belgia, France and Germany . . . (I.i.18–21, 24–9)

At this stage, however, constitutional sanction is still important to
Caesar, and he seeks a resolution in the Senate permitting him to bring
his army into Rome. The first act of the play presents a full-dress debate
unique in Jacobean drama for its subtlety but typical of actual procedure
in public assemblies at all times and places. A well-known maxim of the
strategist von Clausewitz described warfare as politics conducted by
other means. Here, on the verge of war, the politics themselves are
fought out by verbal tactics analogous to military moves. Metellus as
the spokesman of Caesar moves the admission into Rome, not of his
forces, but of his rival Pompey's, in order to establish a precedent for
the entry of Caesar's army. Cato, the elder statesman of the Senate who
in fact sees Pompey as the protector of the republic, blocks the precedent by professing to fear the threat to liberty represented by Pompey's
troops. Caesar's pretext for bringing in the troops is the survival of
supporters of Catiline, the rebel whose attempted *coup d'état* had recently

been put down. The danger from the Catiline faction is magnified by Metellus and minimised by Cato. Caesar rises, ostensibly to argue his disinterested patriotism, in fact to boast his military prowess with a long list of conquests. Pompey replies, disclaiming all ambition, but furnishing an equally impressive account of his own victories. The motion is changed to a resolution for the admission of both armies. Metellus begins to read the bill, but it is snatched from him by one of Cato's supporters. He tries to recite it from memory, but Cato puts a hand over his mouth so that he cannot speak. Politics is already merging with warfare, and the fact is emphasized by the presence at the doors of Caesar's armed thugs. In the ensuing uproar Caesar calls on them to eject Cato. Swords are drawn; the two military rivals abandon constitutional sparring for outright abuse; the meeting ends with shouts of 'War!' from Caesar's ruffians and calls from the consuls for Pompey to defend peace. From now on verbal polemic passes directly into armed conflict.

While interest in the first act is centred on the political crisis, the characters of the main antagonists have begun to emerge. Chapman's Caesar is very different from Shakespeare's senile tyrant. Ruthless, energetic, self-confident, he stands at the height of his powers. Even his disease of epilepsy is ascribed to the physiological effect of ambition; he suffers from 'a spirit too great for all his body's passages to serve it' (I.ii.247–8). Pompey, in spite of his military record, is less sure of himself and already aware that fortune is on Caesar's side. The dominant figure is Cato, the champion of free institutions, who combines moral authority with an adroit mastery of what we should now call parliamentary tactics. Caesar, persuaded that Cato cannot be won over by honours and rewards, had ordered his hooligans to bar his entry to the Senate; characteristically Cato forced his way through at the head of his friends, remarking 'Where fit place is not given, it must be taken' (I.ii.22). There is little in his conduct during this first act to suggest the unworldly philosopher or pre-Christian saint. His principles are bound up with a firm belief in 'heaven's justice', but in this he does not differ from the other characters; what marks him out is his robust assertion that neither the gods nor any earthly power is to be feared by good men. Once warfare has taken the place of debate, Cato's role becomes subsidiary and he is removed from the stage until the fighting ends, but his influence is exerted on Pompey from a distance, advising him, for practical as well as moral reasons, to avoid battle with his adversary.

Through the middle acts of the play, in the vicissitudes of civil war, attention shifts from political issues as such to Chapman's second major concern, the inner world of the two military contestants Caesar and Pompey. Objectively viewed, Caesar is without question the emergent dictator whose triumph must bring the destruction of liberty. But his own view of his motivations makes a more complex impression. Caesar's egotism only functions through a complete identification of his personal ambition with the public good. In his own eyes he is the saviour of his country. Accusations of tyranny rankle and disturb his self-esteem. Unlike the conventional 'statist' of Jacobean drama, Chapman's Caesar is not an amoral cynic; with evident sincerity he prays to the gods for success:

> that my use of it
> May wipe the hateful and unworthy stain
> Of Tyrant from my temples, and exchange it
> For fautor of my country ...   (III.ii.113-16)

Yet while persuading himself that his conduct is determined by virtue, in action he seeks the main chance. Having been defeated at Dyrrhachium, he sends peace proposals to Pompey; they are necessary to gain time, and meanwhile, with characteristic daring, he crosses the straits in a storm to bring over reinforcements. Preparing by every means for new battles, he is nevertheless convinced that his real aim is to end the war. On every occasion where nothing is to be lost by it, he seeks to appear magnanimous. He fosters an ideal image of himself; success brings no inner satisfaction unless it confirms this. But the political world will not allow egotism and altruism to co-exist; Caesar's inner tragedy is the fact that in the end the success he serves will shatter the image by which he lives. For Pompey, the conflict between principle and ambition takes a different form. He profoundly longs to achieve the Stoic stance of indifference to adversity, to seek freedom of mind regardless of fortune. He claims that he desires no praise should he succeed, and will accept no blame should fate prove hostile. His satellite kings urge him on with Senecan aphorisms:

EPIRUS: Free minds like dice fall square whate'er the cost,
IBERIA: Who on himself sole stands, stands solely fast.
THRACE: He's never down whose mind still fights aloft.
CILICIA: Who cares for up or down, when all's but thought?   (III.i.36-9)

Yet in practice, so long as success seems possible, Pompey cannot live up to his principles. The arrival of reinforcements leads him to pray for fortune's favour. Advised by Cato to avoid battle, he nevertheless decides not to call Caesar's bluff and negotiate for peace. Warned by a succession of ill omens, he is unable to face the taunt of cowardice from his own men, and gives orders for the battle at Pharsalia, knowing in his heart that 'the day was lost before 'twas fought'. Only after decisive defeat does Pompey at last become victor over himself, renouncing 'the world's false loves and airy honours'. Henceforth he is determined to seek only human values, to become neither a Pompey nor a Caesar, but a man. In the event, however, the world will allow neither of these 'fools of fortune' to be men. If Caesar's self-image is destroyed by success, Pompey's existence is ended by failure.

With Caesar's victory at Pharsalia, the play enters upon a third phase, which explores, through the main characters, man's universal condition. Pompey and Cato are not seen as political or military leaders but as individuals poised between the world and whatever reality may be thought to transcend it. In the last act Chapman departed from the facts of history to present a reunion between the fugitive Pompey and his wife Cornelia on the island of Lesbos. It is one of his most poignant scenes, irradiated with calm and serenity, and all the more impressive for the grave simplicity of its speech and imagery. Too late, though they are not aware of it, Pompey and Cornelia have both discovered the supreme importance of purely human values. Testing his wife in disguise, Pompey asks her:

'Could you submit yourself cheerfully to your husband, supposing him fallen?' She replies: 'If he submit himself cheerfully to his fortune.' – 'Tis the greatest greatness in the world you undertake.'
'I would be so great, if he were.'
'In supposition.'
'In fact.'
He removes his disguise: 'I am cheerfully fallen; be cheerful.'
'I am, and welcome, as the world was closed
    In these embraces.'   (V.i.149ff.)
The true world seems indeed closed in their embrace. For a few ecstatic minutes they are allowed to believe that they have transcended fortune, history, the universe itself:

> We now are like
> The two poles propping heaven, on which heaven moves,
> And they are fixed and quiet; being above
> All motion far, we rest above the heavens.   (V.i.194–7)

Then the emissaries of Ptolemy, Caesar's ally, break in upon their

The Tragedy of State

peace. Pompey is led off-stage, hacked by their swords and mortally wounded. He staggers back covered with blood, to upbraid the gods in his dying speech for permitting this end to one who has fought in their cause. His sufferings are theirs, he cries:

> after this,
> Who will adore or serve the deities ?   (V.i.262–3)

Throughout the play, fortune and the gods have been invoked by all the contestants. The issue makes a mockery of any trust in their handling of human affairs. Fortune has favoured Caesar, though his victory means the end of human freedom. Pompey, in the days when he thought only of his own ambitions, had been successful; when he fought for his country's good, he was defeated. Even Cato questions the workings of heavenly providence; he is answered by Athenodorus that the gods' wills are unfathomable; for man, it is enough to present their virtues after death untainted by the earth.

> For this giant world,
> Let's not contend with it, when heaven itself
> Fails to reform it...
> A heap 'tis of digested villainy,
> Virtue in labour with eternal chaos,
> Press'd to a living death, and rack'd beneath it,
> Her throes unpitied...   (V.ii.76–8, 80–3)

Such a creed, based on the irremediable corruption of the world, is far removed from the optimism of traditional Christianity.[15] While Chapman in the late scenes of the play allows the Stoic Cato to argue for the immortality of the spirit and even the resurrection of the body, such belief in an afterlife by no means resolves the antinomy between heaven and earth, spirit and nature, that is reinforced by the whole tragic outcome.

For all his metaphysical reasonings, Cato's actions and responses are governed by the primary urge of his life: his aspiration to freedom. So long as tyranny could be fought, he had opposed it; when neither words nor arms could serve him, he chose suicide as a deliberate act of defiance. His conduct is out of accord with any notion of him as a Christian martyr born before his time. There is indeed little of the saint about the fiery old republican, who in the first scene had clapped a hand over Metellus' mouth to prevent him from moving the bill that would admit Caesar's army into Rome, and in the last scene rages at the servants for not bringing him his sword, threatening 'I'll break your lips ope.' Cato

[74]

dies because he will not beg his life of Caesar, who is himself no better than an outlaw or a murderer. At the point of death he looks forward not to heavenly bliss, but to reunion with his former comrades, the brave consuls who had anticipated him in their suicides after Caesar's victory. Not as saint, not as sage, but in the spirit of a Dantesque Ulysses, Cato goes forward to explore the after-life. Having travelled far and seen much, he seeks at last a direct encounter with the enigmatic powers that rule the world.

> Now wing thee, dear soul, and receive her, heaven,
> The earth, the air and seas I know, and all
> The joys and horrors of their peace and wars,
> And now will see the gods' state, and the stars.   (V.ii.158–61)

The final tragedy is Caesar's, who had hoped to give grace to his triumph by a generous pardon for Cato and a show of mercy towards Pompey. Arriving too late, he finds Cato dead, and is driven to exclaim:

> All my late conquest and my life's whole acts
> Most crown'd, most beautified, are blasted all.   (V.ii.180–1)

To quote Chapman's preface, Caesar is 'in spite of all his fortune, without his victory victor'. But worse is in store. Pompey's head is brought to him by the envoys of Ptolemy in the hope of currying favour. He recoils with horror from the shameful sight. Desperately trying to exculpate himself, he gives orders for the emissaries to be tortured to death. As for Cato, a 'sumptuous tomb' is to be given him and a statue erected in his honour. The historical Caesar did none of these things; but even such gestures, accorded him by Chapman, are of little avail. No torture for his allies, no statues to his enemies, can restore Caesar's own fallen image. Cato's last words had been: 'Just men are only free, the rest are slaves.' Caesar survives, a slave of policy, ruling slaves. At the end of the play there is only one man to whom he turns, only one enemy he has reconciled. Pathetically he thanks him, saying 'You do me infinite honour.' The remark carries its own historical irony, for that man is Brutus.

NOTES

1. *Shakespeare Survey* 20 (1967), pp. 113–20.

2. Weimann, *loc. cit.*, p. 116.

3. *Bellum Catilinarium*, chapter X (translated J. C. Rolfe, Loeb Classical Library, 1920). Cited by Joseph Allen Bryant Jr., '*Catiline* and the Nature

of Jonson's Tragic Fable', *Papers of the Modern Language Association* LXIX (1) (1954), p. 267; reprinted in *Ben Jonson: Critical Essays* (Twentieth Century Views), ed. Jonas A. Barish (1963), p. 149.

4. Interesting recent discussions of the relationship of history to Renaissance tragedy appear in Bryant's article (see note 3), Jonas A. Barish's Introduction to Ben Jonson's *Sejanus, The Yale Ben Jonson*, 1965, and Hibbard's 'Chapman: Tragedy and the Providential View of History' (see III, note 10, p. 56). Hibbard traces the decline of 'the providential idea' in history and tragedy alike, and the rise in the same period of secular interpretations to historical development and tragic experience. Thus the 'historical revolution' coincided with the 'dramatic revolution': Shakespeare's *Richard III*, based on 'providential history', was followed by *King Lear*, where divine justice was questioned and the action presented, in Machiavellian fashion, 'what men do, and not what they ought to do'.

5. 'The really important and interesting and relevant political lessons were those concerned with *princes*. It was this that turned the attention away from republican Rome to monarchical Rome: the Rome of the Twelve Caesars and their successors . . . in sixteenth-century Europe republics happened to be rather rare . . . An occasional eccentric enthusiasm for one or both of the two Brutuses does not weigh against the fact that it was the busts of the Twelve Caesars that decorated almost every palace in Europe.' T. J. B. Spencer, 'Shakespeare and the Elizabethan Romans', *Shakespeare Survey* 10 (1957), pp. 30–1; reprinted in Maurice Charney, *Discussions of Shakespeare's Roman Plays* (1965), pp. 6–7.

6. Junius J. Brutus (pseudonym), *A Defence of Liberty Against Tyrants*, ed. Harold J. Laski (1924), pp. 183–4. The author based his case against the absolute right of kings upon both Old Testament precedents and republican traditions. He affirmed that kings were made by the people, who had delegated to them their power and sovereignty; that not only tyrannical usurpers, but 'the prince who applied himself to nothing but his peculiar profits and pleasures, or to those ends which most readily conduce thereunto, who contemns and perverts all laws, who uses his subjects more cruelly that the barbarous enemy would do, he may truly and really be called a tyrant' (p. 143). Examples were also drawn from Roman history: 'A tyrant tops off those ears which grow higher than the rest of the corn, especially where virtue makes them most conspicuously eminent; oppresses by calumnies and fraudulent practices the principal officers of the state; gives out reports of intended conspiracies against himself, that he might have some colourable pretext to cut them off; witness Tiberius, Maximinius, and others, who spared not their own kinsmen, cousins, and brothers' (p. 185).

7. Machiavelli relates that Olgiato and his companions Lampugnano and Visconti had been educated in Milan by their tutor Cola Montano, who

instilled into them not only classical Latin but a reverence for the virtues of republican Rome. 'He did his best to show them that the most famous men had been produced in republics, not brought up under princes; that republics cherish virtue, while princes destroy it' (*Historia Fiorentina*, lib. vii, chapter 6). Lorenzino, who escaped from Florence after the assassination of Duke Alessandro in 1537, was acclaimed by his fellow-exiles as 'the Tyrannicide' and 'the Tuscan Brutus'. Verses and encomiums were composed in his honour. (Varchi, *Storia Fiorentina*, lib. xv; reprinted in Paul Dimoff, *La Genèse de Lorenzaccio*). Hans Baron, *The Crisis of the Early Italian Renaissance* (1955), chapter 3, describes the rise of the republican interpretation of history, as opposed to Dante's monarchist opinions. It was initiated by Bruni's *Dialogi* and *Laudatio Florentinae Urbis* in the early fifteenth century, which eulogised Brutus and condemned both Caesar and Caesarism.

8. Translated by G. Bullough, *Narrative and Dramatic Sources of Shakespeare*, Vol. V (1964), p. 179. The passages that follow also make use of Bullough's translations and line references.

9. Cinthio, *Cleopatra* (1583), V.6 (Bullough V, p. 356).

10. Bryant sees in Jonson's Roman plays 'a tragic action with the state itself taking the role of a tragic protagonist. Jonson . . . was the first to make drama serve as a medium for presenting the tragedy of a whole state.' (*Ben Jonson*, ed. Barish, p. 157.)

11. Contemporary audiences would have noted the parallel to the public burning of satires and other 'seditious' works by order of Archbishop Whitgift in 1598.

12. Ben Jonson: *Sejanus*, ed. Jonas A. Barish, *The Yale Ben Jonson* (1965), Introduction, pp. 20–1. My interpretation of *Sejanus* is much indebted to this edition.

13. Rees, *The Tragedies of George Chapman*, pp. 142–9.

14. Ornstein, *The Moral Vision of Jacobean Tragedy*, p. 80.

15. Roy W. Battenhouse, 'Chapman and the Nature of Man', *ELH* XII (1945), pp. 87–107 (reprinted in *Elizabethan Essays*, ed. Kaufmann, pp. 134–52), argues that Chapman, like Greville, believed in a Platonic 'two-story universe', where nature was subject to fate and rational or spiritual man to Providence. 'The logic of Chapman and Greville is thus the logic of despair, moving dialectically from nature to grace – nature being understood in more or less Machiavellian terms, and grace being equated with Platonic and Stoic idealism' (ed. Kaufmann, p. 147). If poets and dramatists were theologians, such interpretations might be sufficient. But a sense of despair at the workings of God and man in a society corrupted by power hardly entitles us to suppose that Chapman labelled the universe as 'Machiavellian', or 'idealist', or some dualistic compound of the two.

Webster:
The White Devil, The Duchess of Malfi

In the sixteenth century the dispatches of the great banking house of Fugger provided the first all-European news service. During the Christmas season of 1585 the Venetian correspondent reported serious disturbances in the old university city of Padua. A band of fifty armed men, led by a certain nobleman, Ludovico Orsini, had invaded the palace of Vittoria, the Duke of Bracciano's young widow, at two o'clock on the morning of December 22nd. The gates had been opened for them; inside they shot down the lady's brother Flaminio and stabbed Vittoria to death without even allowing her time to finish her prayers. Padua was stirred at the crime, in which the hidden hand of the Duke of Florence was suspected. The students armed themselves and paraded through the streets shouting for justice. In alarm the government of Venice, which ruled the city, sent troops and cannon to attack the assassins, who had barricaded themselves in Orisini's family residence. After a struggle in which a number of the band were killed, the rest surrendered. Three were torn to pieces by the citizenry, others were taken and hanged. Lodovico Orsini himself confessed that he had performed the crime 'at the command of great personages'. He was sentenced to death by strangling; but since he claimed a nobleman's privilege, the execution was carried out in private. Moreover, a gift of fifty crowns to the executioner ensured him a speedy and relatively painless death.

Such were the happenings on which Webster based his tragedy *The White Devil*, performed early in 1612. Behind them lay a tangle of crimes and intrigues described in 109 extant accounts preserved in libraries of Italy, Austria, England and America.[1] None of these accounts exactly coincides with the story of Webster's play; nor is it to be expected that they should, since *The White Devil* made no claim to historical accuracy. But it is generally thought that Webster drew his information mainly from the same Italian source as the Fugger correspondent in Venice. Not only the facts he used, but a number of details he altered have left their traces. For example, the fictitious Lodovico is arrested in Vittoria's palace straight after the crime, and we are not told how he died; but in the first scene of the play he remarks:

> I have seen some ready to be executed
> Give pleasant looks, and money, and grow familiar
> With the knave hangman . . .   (I.i.54–6)

This looks very much like Webster's reminiscence of Lodovico Orsini's actual conduct before his execution in Venice. In the play Vittoria is not murdered while praying; indeed we would hardly associate her with such pieties, were it not that in Act V Scene vi she enters carrying a book, to be greeted by Flamineo with the words 'What, are you at your prayers?' Again, the real-life Bracciano suffered greatly from an ulcer in the leg. Nothing is said of this in the play, but in the course of his quarrel with Vittoria in Act IV she uses the striking metaphor for her love of him:

> I had a limb corrupted to an ulcer,
> But I have cut it off, and now I'll go
> Weeping to heaven on crutches.   (IV.ii.121–33)

As for the main motivations of the tragedy, these do not depart far from the essential facts. Bracciano was responsible for the death of his wife, sister of the Duke of Florence, – though this crime had taken place some years before his affair with Vittoria – as well as the murder of Vittoria's husband, nephew to a cardinal who soon afterwards became Pope Paul IV. With the open marriage of Bracciano and Vittoria the hostility of two powerful forces in state and church was irrevocably sealed. Bracciano died in suspicious circumstances while taking a cure on Lake Garda, and next month Vittoria and her brother were murdered in Padua, almost certainly at the instigation of the Duke of Florence.

Since this chain of murders and reprisals was a matter of historical fact, occurring in Webster's own lifetime, one need not be surprised that it served as material for drama. Nevertheless the picture of a society where such happenings could easily take place, and of eminent figures who could proceed to such crimes, hardly squared with the past as seen through the eyes of some nostalgic critics. Accordingly Webster, and not the world of his time, has been blamed for moral nihilism and morbidity. T. S. Eliot summed him up as 'a very great literary and dramatic genius directed toward chaos'.[2] Ian Jack was more explicit.

Webster's drama, he objected, 'contains no convincing statement of the *positive* aspect of the doctrine of Degree . . . It is not surprising that a mind as unbalanced as Webster's should have allowed the Machiavellian ideal to usurp the place in his thought which a more conservative poet would have reserved for Degree.'[3] Had Webster's mind been properly balanced – that is to say, suitably conservative – he would, Jack implies, have seen the Renaissance world as a radiant vision of God-given harmonies. The facts of tyranny, intrigue, hypocrisy and violence would have been neatly conceptualized into an unhealthy 'Machiavellian ideal', before being banished from the writer's antiseptic brain. – Needless to say, no serious dramatist of the Jacobean age reacted in this manner. On the other hand there is some need to consider what artistic, as distinct from moral, purpose may have shaped Webster's decision to return to the Italian settings of Marston and Tourneur and to the slightly old-fashioned mode of the revenge play.

We shall best understand what is distinctive in Webster's approach if we start by noting what it has in common with this earlier kind of drama. I have to disagree with J. R. Brown, the very able editor of *The White Devil*, when he describes the play's structure as 'loose and rambling, a gothic aggregation rather than a steady exposition and development'.[4] *The White Devil* is basically well designed, building up steadily from act to act, with a minor climax in Act III and a full revenge catastrophe at the end. Acts I and II present very concisely the love intrigue of Bracciano and Vittoria, the double murder of his wife and her husband, and the arousing of the forces that will finally avenge it. Act III is centred upon the trial of Vittoria: the first, inconclusive blow struck by the revengers. In Act IV the quarrel between Bracciano and Vittoria brings out the inherent precariousness of their relationship, while the revengers plan the decisive stroke that will ensure the destruction of the lovers. The last act brings the second wave of revenge, the murders of Bracciano, Vittoria and their go-between Flamineo, the deaths of the revengers, and the final restoration of order. In addition, there are some secondary elaborations, such as the installation of the new Pope, and the recurrent appearance of the six lieger ambassadors. In terms of plot-mechanics these are dispensable, but they contribute to the total thematic effect. On the other hand there is brilliant economy in presenting the double murder of Isabella and Camillo through dumb-shows, and the instigation to this crime through the narration of a dream. Viewed in terms of the revenge play tradition,

The White Devil shows most of the familiar type-figures and relationships. The norm of authority is represented by Giovanni, the young son of Bracciano by his first wife, who in the end takes charge and punishes the wrongdoers. Bracciano occupies the position of the traditional tyrant, the unscrupulous slave of passion, commiting murder and adultery and employing Flamineo as his henchman. A bad father, an unfaithful husband, his vices are offset by the presence of such virtuous characters as his son Giovanni and his wife Isabella, while his mistress Vittoria is contrasted to her mother Cornelia, and Flamineo to his brother Marcello. Ranged against them are the revengers, Francisco Duke of Florence and the Cardinal Monticelso, later to become Pope, with Lodovico and his companions as their instruments. In correspondence with the conventional masque that converted the tyrant's festivities into a scene of carnage, the revengers appear at Bracciano's marriage celebrations in the bizarre disguises of a Moorish warrior and two Hungarian Capuchins. After they have enacted a suitably horrific vengeance, the boy Giovanni restores authority, ordering that the malefactors be imprisoned and tortured.

Yet in spite of the conventional organization, the current of sympathy flows in an *opposite* direction to that of the earlier revenge drama. Bracciano, in the situation of the tyrant, is attractively virile and courageous, passionate as a lover, scornful of his dangerous opponents. The advanced middle age, the corpulence and ulcerated leg of the real-life Bracciano do not appear in Webster's character, who gives the impression of a man at the peak of his energies. Flamineo, his accomplice and pander, takes over the intellectual acuteness and caustic wit usually reserved for the revenger, and provides a satirical commentary on the vices of the great. He appears as the son of an impoverished family made up of his sister Vittoria, brother Marcello, and their widowed mother Cornelia. There is an obvious parallel to Vindice and his family in *The Revenger's Tragedy*; but while Vindice only pretends to solicit his sister Castiza by way of testing her virtue, Flamineo wholeheartedly accepts his mission as the Duke's agent, while Vittoria is entirely willing to take Bracciano as her lover. In Tourneur's play the poor and virtuous family unites against the self-destructive dynasty of the tyrant; in *The White Devil* the family is divided, with Flamineo and Vittoria juxtaposed to Marcello and Cornelia. While the wrongdoers have colour and vitality, the innocent characters are faded and submissive. Isabella as the deserted wife evokes a limited degree of pity in much the same way as Shakespeare's Octavia in *Antony and Cleopatra*,

[81]

after whom she is probably modelled.[5] Like Octavia, her alternations of mute reproach and ostentatious self-effacement make no firm impression. Cornelia briefly arrests attention in the first act, but she is soon silenced by Flamineo's withering scorn. Reappearing in Act V, she is given a contrived pathos by Webster's plagiarisms from the speeches of the mad Ophelia in *Hamlet*; but the device is so forced that it militates against a sympathetic response. As for Camillo, Vittoria's husband, in life an agreeable young man, he appears in the play as a ridiculous cuckold, a suitable butt for Flamineo's gulling. On the other hand, the revengers, Monticelso and Francisco, Cardinal and Grand Duke, are neither poor nor oppressed, but specimens of the corrupt statesman inveighed against by all the dramatists of the age. The arraignment of Vittoria is a flagrant travesty of justice, in which the Cardinal acts as both prosecutor and judge and condemns her on palpably flimsy evidence. The outcome is that Vittoria, sentenced as a whore to live in a 'house of convertites', dominates the court, and turns the charges back upon her accusers:

> It shall not be a house of convertites –
> My mind shall make it honester to me
> Than the Pope's palace, and more peaceable
> Than thy soul, though thou art a cardinal.   (III.ii.289–92)

Francisco is similarly defied by Bracciano when he threatens to use his military force if Vittoria is not given up:

> All thy loud cannons, and thy borrow'd Switzers,
> Thy galleys, nor thy sworn confederates
> Durst not supplant her.   (II.i.60–3)

Crafty and hypocritical, the revengers are more repulsive than the wrongdoers they punish. Francisco selects his instruments of vengeance from the Cardinal's 'black book' of criminals. Compiled by intelligencers for the purposes of blackmail rather than justice, it is the only book one sees in that ecclesiastical dignitary's hands. Even the boy Giovanni, Bracciano's son but Francisco's nephew, is a questionable figure. Ostensibly the embodiment of a better order, Flamineo notes that 'he hath his uncle's villanous look already', and cryptically remarks that 'the wolf and raven Are very pretty fools when they are young' (V.iv.30, 35–6). There is no assurance that Giovanni, grown to manhood, will prove better than Francisco or any other of the 'princes' and 'great men' who make up the world of the play.

In fact it is to this omnipresent world of corruption that we must look if we are to understand the cross-currents of *The White Devil*. In form a revenge tragedy, it rejects the clear polarities of vice and virtue, oppression and revolt, which set up the moral tension of this class of drama. Innocent and virtuous characters do indeed appear and offset the wickedness of the major figures by their presence and their comments. But they have no vitality on the stage. In the world of *The White Devil*, as in the world of Jonson's *Sejanus*, their parts are condemned to be passive. Virtue is allowed, is even encouraged, to speak out; but it has no field of action; and it is in the nature of drama that the audience's sympathies are engaged by energy, not passive endurance. Still, it oversimplifies the effect if we only see this as an inversion of conventional sympathy, or respond to the parts of Bracciano, Vittoria and Flamineo with unqualified admiration. Again and again their conduct and their attitudes are set in a wider frame of reference. This is supplied not by the traditional virtues, but by the universal evil of which they form a part. When Bracciano in his jealousy vents his anger on Flamineo, he becomes identified with all the other type-despots of society.

BRACCIANO: Do you know me?
FLAMINEO: O my lord! methodically.
As in this world there are degrees of evils:
So in this world there are degrees of devils.
You're a great duke; I your poor secretary.
I do look now for a Spanish fig, or an Italian
sallet daily. . . .   (IV.ii.56–61)

In the end Flamineo and his sister recognize themselves as the victims of their rulers. Vittoria's last words are

O happy they that never saw the court,
Nor ever knew great men but by report.   (V.vi.261–2)

Flamineo's dying speech cautions those who enjoy court favour:

'Let all that belong to great men remember th'old wives tradition, to be like the lions i'th' Tower on Candlemas Day, to mourn if the sun shine, for fear of the pitiful remainder of winter to come.'   (V.vi.265–8)

This final recognition is prepared for from the first lines of the play. Guilty and innocent alike are the victims of power; it is in the light of this truth that the moral ambivalences are resolved. A clear instance may be seen in the sinuous dramatic unfolding of Act I scene ii. Bracciano's desperation in love is balanced by Flamineo's glib assurances that Vittoria will presently receive him, that her chambermaid Zanche has been 'dealt with', and that he has nothing to fear from her jealous husband. While romance is offset by cynicism, the farcical presentation of Camillo swings sympathy back to the lovers. Yet when Bracciano and Vittoria do meet, they are flanked by the sceptical presence of the two go-betweens Flamineo and Zanche; and behind these, providing yet another discordant effect, stands Cornelia, horrified by the immoral compliance of her son and daughter. She breaks up the lovers' assignation, denouncing the wickedness of her children. For once even Vittoria is overcome with guilt and leaves abruptly. But Cornelia's virtue is not the final criterion of values. When she asks, 'because we are poor, shall we be vicious?' Flamineo rounds on her with a telling account of the social circumstances that have made him what he is:

> Pray, what means have you
> To keep me from the galleys, or the gallows?
> My father prov'd himself a gentleman,
> Sold all's land, and like a fortunate fellow,
> Died ere the money was spent. You brought me up
> At Padua I confess, where I protest
> For want of means, – the university judge me, –
> I have been fain to heel my tutor's stockings
> At least seven years: conspiring with a beard
> Made me a graduate, – then to this duke's service:
> I visited the court, whence I return'd, . . .
> But not a suit the richer, – and shall I,
> Having a path so open and so free
> To my preferment, still retain your milk
> In my pale forehead?   (I.ii.315-30)

The total effect of this scene is not to focus attention on the illicit romance, on Camillo's marital rights, on the cynicism of the go-betweens, or on Cornelia's virtue, but to place all these in the wider context of a society where declassed intellectuals find the only alternative to galleys, or gallows, in serving without scruple the desires of their rulers.

Throughout *The White Devil* the suffocating ambience of power and oppression is insisted on as the atmosphere in which all the characters move and have their being. Scene after scene reinforces the implication and sums up the theme in sententious couplets which have an impersonal choric effect. Lodovico, the arch-ruffian of the play, speaks for all when he comments:

> Great men sell sheep, thus to be cut in pieces,
> When first they have shorn them bare and sold their fleeces.
> (I.i.62–3)

According to Flamineo,

> who knows policy and her true aspect,
> Shall find her ways winding and indirect. (I.ii.353–4)

The conjurer who presents Bracciano's murders in dumb-show ends Act II with the aphorism:

> Both flowers and weeds spring when the sun is warm,
> And great men do great good, or else great harm. (II.ii.56–7)

And again, more pointedly, Flamineo remarks:

> There's but three Furies found in spacious hell,
> But in a great man's breast three thousand dwell. (IV.iii.152–3)

Through a mass of fragmentary images and conceits the iniquities of the age fall into a kaleidoscopic pattern. Spanish reprisals in the Netherlands are the substance of Flamineo's simile: 'When knaves come to preferment they rise as gallowses are raised i'th' Low Countries, one upon another's shoulders' (II.i.320–2). Monticelso the Cardinal alludes to

> those tributes i'th' Low Countries paid,
> Exactions upon meat, drink, garments, sleep;
> Ay, even on man's perdition, his sin. (III.ii.86–8)

The defeated Irish rebels selling their comrades' heads to the English queen's officers; the forty thousand pedlars of impoverished Poland; the soldiers back from serving against the Turk, with only enough in the way of pension to buy themselves wooden legs and fresh plasters –

> the beggary of courtiers,
> The discontent of churchmen, want of soldiers,
> And all the creatures that hang manacled,
> Worse than strappadoed, on the lowest felly
> Of Fortune's wheel... (III.iii.92–6)

all these are the broken humanity of Renaissance Europe. Such a civilization has no tears to shed at Cornelia's pious laments, no moral indignation to waste over Bracciano's individual sins.

At the other extreme, the hollow pomps and splendours of greatness are displayed with calculated irony. Six ambassadors to the Papal court look on at the hypocritical trial of Vittoria and see her condemned as a whore. They proceed to the Pope's investiture, wearing the stately habits of their chivalric orders as Knights of the Holy Ghost, the Annunciation, the Garter dedicated to Saint George, and so on, to hear the new Pope as his first act in office decree the excommunication of Bracciano and Vittoria. Unperturbed, the ambassadors presently arrive in Padua, still wearing their emblems of sanctity and honour, to attend the wedding festivities of an excommunicated duke and a sentenced whore. Joining in the celebrations they fight at the barriers, imitating the tournaments of an obsolete chivalry, while Bracciano agonizes in his poisoned helmet. Also present at the wedding are Francisco, Lodovico and Gasparo; Francisco disguised as a glamorous Moorish warrior, the others as two Hungarian noblemen who have served against 'the enemies of Christ' and are entering 'the strict order of the Capuchins'. Outwardly simulating the nobility and sanctity of Christendom, the revengers in a fiendish parody of the last rites pronounce curses on the dying Bracciano, then murder Vittoria and Flamineo. Webster has been blamed for crowding his play with irrelevant spectacle. Much of it, as here, gives dramatic expression to the overiding theme of a corrupt society.

It is understandable therefore that *The White Devil* should be a drama without heroes. The flamboyant courage of Bracciano and Vittoria, the caustic intellect of Flamineo, evoke a measure of admiration, but this does not imply a new ethic of amoralism. *Through darkness diamonds spread their richest light*: it is the depth of the surrounding darkness, not the quality of the gems, that chiefly concerns us. Like Jonson's *Sejanus*, Webster's satirical tragedy looks beyond individuals to the society that has shaped them. Both plays treat revenge as the action of greater malefactors against lesser ones, and allow virtue no more than a passive part. Both take as their theme the debasement of a whole civilization. Jonson's tragic protagonist is not Sejanus but imperial Rome. In Webster's play too there are in the final analysis no tragic heroes or heroines. The White Devil is not Vittoria Corombona but Renaissance Europe.

The Duchess of Malfi, written about a year later, was clearly a re-shaping of *The White Devil*. Again the story was taken from Italian history, some seventy years before the events dramatized in the previous play. Again Webster based the action on a vendetta resulting from an unconventional match, leading to the deaths of both the revengers and their victims. The affinities are obvious between Duke Ferdinand and the Cardinal and the Duke of Florence and Cardinal of *The White Devil*; between Bosola the secret agent and Flamineo the pander; between the pair of lovers, the Duchess and Antonio, and Vittoria and Bracciano. Further correspondences may be found in the structure, the infusion of satire and sententious comment, the appearance at the end of a child heir offering promise of a better order. Nevertheless, *The Duchess of Malfi* is essentially different in its perspective, its field of concern, and its tragic effect.

Some of the reasons for this difference have been well brought out by J. R. Brown in his edition of the play. The setting of a small court, the concentration on immediate and topical abuses, the story itself as 'a syndrome for contemporary issues': all show Webster directing his attention upon England.[6] The court of Amalfi presents in miniature the court of Whitehall, with its adventurers, its feverish pulling of strings for office and promotion, its heedless and heartless pursuit of privilege. At the time when the play was being written, James I had dispensed with the responsible chief minister Cecil, and placed the entire control of the state in the hands of his young favourite Robert Carr. The Privy Council had become a mere rubber stamp for arbitrary personal rule. Honours were openly bought and sold; marriages and divorces were steps to political influence. In this atmosphere normal human relationships were stifled. The pitiful case of Lady Arabella Stuart must surely have been present in the minds of audiences seeing *The Duchess of Malfi*. This modest, unassuming lady had the misfortune to have been born the king's cousin, and therefore a possible claimant to the throne. For years she had lived quietly at court, rejecting all attempts to involve her in the various conspiracies against James. Then she made the mistake of falling in love with William Seymour, who was also of royal blood. Their secret marriage was punished by the imprisonment of both husband and wife. Each managed to escape, and sailed separately for Ostend, hoping to be reunited and live in peace abroad as private persons. Seymour landed, but Lady Arabella was captured at sea and brought back to spend the rest of her days in prison. It is not strange that in *The Duchess of Malfi* the affairs of England, and in particular the inner life of the victims of state and their persecutors, shape the world of the play beneath its Italian surface, and give to its tragic content a more personal and sympathetic quality than in *The White Devil*.

The difference of approach is immediately suggested in the opening lines. *The White Devil* begins with a banishment, *The Duchess of Malfi* with a homecoming. In the former play Lodovico rages to his fellow ruffians against fortune, the gods, courtly reward and punishment: here, Antonio speaks to his friend Delio of the reformed court of France, purged by its king of 'sycophants', of 'dissolute and infamous persons', and governed by a council who dare freely Inform him of the corruption of the times'. Instead of the imprecations of *The White Devil*, ranging over the abuses of the whole Renaissance world, this play offers the contrast of a changed society in one country, which may set a precedent to others. The description is visually reinforced by Antonio's appearance, distinctively dressed as 'a very formal Frenchman'. The scene opens out into a presentation of the unregenerate court of Malfi, introducing in turn its malcontent Bosola, the Cardinal, Ferdinand, and at last the Duchess. For over three hundred lines action is minimal, while the audience observes these key figures, characterized by Antonio, Delio, and for a while Bosola. The Cardinal and Ferdinand, it is learned, are

> 'like plum-trees, that grow crooked over standing pools; they are rich, and o'erladen with fruit, but none but crows, pies, and caterpillars feed on them' (I.i.49–52).

Crookedness, stagnancy and favouritism typify the great eminences of the play, whose one action so far, the appointment of Bosola to spy upon the Duchess, is itself tortuous and corrupt. Again, a positive contrast is struck in Antonio's ardent praise of the Duchess, which dwells not on her beauty but on the charm of her manner and the chastity of her conduct:

> ... in that look
> There speaketh so divine a continence
> As cuts off all lascivious, and vain hope.
> Her days are practis'd in such noble virtue
> That sure her nights – nay more, her very sleeps –
> Are more in heaven than other ladies' shrifts ...
> All her particular worth grows to this sum:
> She stains the time past, lights the age to come.[7]
>
> (I.i.198–203, 208–9)

The opening scene, with its close-range focus on the principal court characters, differs sharply from the negative panorama of *The White Devil*. While the evils of policy are embodied in the Duke and Cardinal, there are positive elements: the presence of Antonio as a living remin-

[88]

der of possible regeneration, and the virtuous influence of the Duchess, who 'lights the age to come'. In this changed perspective the revenge plot operates with a different effect from that of the earlier play. In *The White Devil* retribution fell upon two adulterous lovers whose first encounter had precipitated a double murder. The revengers were indeed less attractive than their victims; but all alike functioned in a moral vacuum created by the political world to which they belonged. In *The Duchess of Malfi* the Duke and Cardinal are motivated solely by their resentment at the innocent marriage of a pair whose virtue is established from the start and who offer the promise of a better way of life. Hence the sympathy of the audience, both moral and instinctive, is ranged on the side of the Duchess and Antonio. The play is in fact a revenge drama only in the sense that Chapman's *Bussy D'Ambois* may be considered one: it presents the vengeance of the leaders of state and church upon those who by their life challenge its inverted values. For Ferdinand and the Cardinal, as for the Guise and Monsieur, 'Reward goes backward, Honour on its head'. In contrast, Antonio the commoner and the Duchess who prefers a marriage of love to the sterile privileges of rank and power may be taken to represent 'man in his native noblesse'.

There would be no need to dwell on these facts were it not for the arguments of some modern critics, whose reading of the play contradicts the impression formed by any audience, Jacobean or contemporary. Just as Marlowe, Shakespeare and Chapman have been re-classified as apologists for 'order and degree', so Webster is in process of being converted from a chaotic, unbalanced 'genius' into the spokesman of a trite orthodoxy. The secret marriage of the widowed Duchess and Antonio is said to have been wanton and irreligious, and their difference of rank to have made it also a shocking violation of degree.[8] For confirmation a hypothetical Jacobean opinion is invoked, unanimously agreed on certain certainties. A sufficient answer to latter-day moralizers might be that audiences in every age admire characters with courage, wit and sincerity; approve of marriage for love, even if it be the second marriage of a girl widowed at twenty; and hate the murderous intrigues of great personages who would turn normal human happiness into misery. Should this reply seem too obvious to be scholarly, one might point out the approval of Webster's contemporaries, Middleton, Rowley and Ford, in the commendatory verses prefixed to the first edition of *The Duchess of Malfi*. The play is described as 'this masterpiece of tragedy'; as for the author,

> Thy epitaph only the title be, –
> Write 'Duchess', that will fetch a tear for thee,
> For who e'er saw this duchess live, and die,
> That could get off under a bleeding eye?

It has been said that the re-marriage of widows, though widespread in all classes, was disapproved of; mention is made of the strictures of Painter in the English translation of Bandello which Webster used as his source. In fact, Painter explicitly defends re-marriage on grounds both of morality and common sense:

> . . . to say the truth,' 'they be not guided by wisdomes lore, which suffer a maiden ripe for marriage to be long vnwedded, or young wife long to liue in widdowes state . . . a great follie it is to build the fantasies of chastitie, amind the follies of worldy pleasures.[9]

As for the violation of 'degree', Painter's characters are their own convincing apologists. They appeal over the heads of established order to God and human decency in justification of the Duchess's decision:

> Is not she at libertie? To whom ought she to make accompt of hir dedes and doings, but to God alone and to hir owne conscience? . . . In this, there is no cause to blame Loue of blindnesse, for all the inequalitie of our houses . . . But from whence issue the Monarches, Princes and greater Lords, but from the naturall and common masse of earth, whereof other men doe come? what maketh these differences betwene those that loue eche other, if not the sottish opinion which we conceiue of greatnesse, and preheminence: as though naturall affections be like to that ordained by the fantasie of men in their lawes extreme . . . I thinke we be the daily slaves of the fond and cruell fantasie of those Tyraunts, which say they have puissance over us; and that straining our will to their tirannie, we be still bound to the chaine like the galley slave.'[10]

There are, it is true, short pietistic insertions in Painter's story which perform an abrupt about-turn in attitude. They are to be found in all this class of *novelle* published with an eye to the new reading public.[11] The object, here as elsewhere, was to provide a sop for the more strait-laced members of the middle class. Had Painter dreamed that this moral façade would be solemnly accepted by literary scholars of the twentieth century, I feel he would have been much amused at their gullibility. As for the main drift of the narrative, it accords with the attitude of Webster's fellow writers and the response of normal theatre-goers in every age.

The Duchess of Malfi is indeed a highly moral play; but its morality does not toady to the prejudices of an establishment. It draws its strength from communal attitudes regardless of historical period, and is implicit in the responses called forth by action, characterization and imagery working in close conjunction. There is a clear difference between the dramatic effect of the secret marriage that ends Act I and the assignation of Bracciano and Vittoria in Act I of *The White Devil*. The equivocal effects do not work in the same way. In *The White Devil* the lovers are flanked by their cynical go-betweens and all are alike condemned by Cornelia. In *The Duchess of Malfi* the maid Cariola is out of sight, and equally out of mind, until she comes forward at the right moment as the indispensable witness to what is in fact a common-law contract of marriage.[12] Meanwhile the couple are alone and sympathy is not deflected by the presence and comments of bystanders. There are no impediments to this marriage of true minds: the Duchess's proposal enhances her dignity and grace; Antonio's replies show deep affection tempered by the caution natural to his situation. While the love scene in *The White Devil* breaks up in discord, in *The Duchess of Malfi* it is crowned by a simple ceremony. Antonio kneels to receive the Duchess's ring as if the accolade of knighthood were bestowed on him, and is raised to join her in the noblesse of nature. The church – represented in this play by the Cardinal – cannot bind faster; instead, the two direct their prayers immediately to heaven.

DUCH: Bless heaven this sacred Gordian, which let violence
         Never untwine.
ANTONIO: And may our sweet affections, like the spheres,
         Be still in motion.
DUCHESS: Quickening, and make
         The like soft music.   (I.i.480–4)

Yet accompanying these affirmations of harmony there are latent discords. The Duchess's proposal of marrage is phrased in terms of making a will; the sheets of the nuptial bed are also winding sheets; her kiss gives Antonio his *quietus*. Images of insanity menace the lovers: Antonio's description of ambition anticipates the mental torments later to be inflicted by Ferdinand:

> Ambition, madam, is a great man's madness,
> That is not kept in chains, and close-pent rooms,
> But in fair lightsome lodgings, and is girt
> With the wild noise of prattling visitants ...   (I.i.420–3)

The sense of impending disaster grows not out of suggestions of inner guilt, but from knowledge of the implacable enmity of the outside world. In *The White Devil* the lovers are never seen at peace with one another. Their precarious union is easily broken; Francisco's ruse in Act IV leads to a rapid flare-up of suspicion and mutual reproach. Bracciano, fatally poisoned, cannot bear Vittoria's presence, and orders her away from his death-bed. In *The Duchess of Malfi* no inner tension upsets the tranquility of the marriage. Affection extends over the years to include both parents and offspring. When leave-taking is forced upon her, the Duchess, who had matched without the ministrations of the established church, puts her trust for reunion in a higher truth: 'in the eternal church, sir, I do hope we shall not part thus' (III.v.71–2). The premonitions of tragedy in Act I come to fulfilment solely through the machinations of external forces. Fears are deepened in Act II through events which by normal expectation should be happy and blessed: the birth of the first child is followed by a terrible horoscope and the kindled anger of the Aragonian brothers. In Act III the birth of further children and the Duchess's revelation to Bosola that the admired Antonio is her husband turns menace into action with the beginning of her enemies' revenge.

The malign forces are partly located in the cosmos of Webster. There is no ambivalence about the nature of human love, but there is an unresolved doubt as to the nature of the universe which shapes its course. As in Chapman, fortune and the stars favour power against virtue. The Duchess and Antonio evoke heaven to bless their match and make it fruitful; she parts from him trusting that the eternal church will bring them together; she dies kneeling to enter heaven's gates. But disaster is predicted for her firstborn son; she is driven to curse the stars; after death, her ghostly echo warns Antonio that he will never see her more; Antonio is killed by chance when Bosola had meant to save him. On the rational plane no causal connection can be found between the malignancy of the cosmos and that of earthly powers. But it is in the way of the creative imagination that the evil of human tyranny should be projected out upon the universe. At the core of the drama, however, evil as well as good is embodied in the individual. In *The White Devil*, where the conspectus took in society as a whole, personal motivation was obvious and unsubtle. The legal hypocrisies of Vittoria's trial, the satirical inversion of piety and chivalry at Bracciano's murder, aroused more attention than the state of mind of the revengers. But in *The Duchess of Malfi* personality is brought into close focus. From this viewpoint again the play has marked affinities with Chapman's *Bussy D'Ambois*. Ferdinand and the Cardinal, like the Guise and Monsieur, give an individual quality to the violence and cunning of state. With both pairs the personal motive is an affront to aristocratic pride of blood. But whereas in *Bussy* the Senecan spirit of tragic fury is infused into the revenge through the choice of a jealous husband as the instrument of murder, there is no counterpart to this role in *The Duchess of Malfi*. The Duchess is faithful, and Bosola who conducts the revenge is merely a hired agent. Accordingly Webster would seem to have galvanized Ferdinand's antipathies of rank by attributing to him the jealous rage of the cuckolded husband Montsurry. The appearance of sexual anger and guilt in a brother-sister relationship results in a pattern of thought and behaviour which modern readers promptly diagnose as a case of sub-conscious incest. Yet it is by no means certain that this was the impression Webster wished to create. Jacobean playwrights were not at all reticent in their treatment of incest, and had he wished Webster could well have made Ferdinand's urges quite explicit. Dramatic construction and tragic effect explain his treatment more convincingly than a quest for psychological complexity beyond the capacity of the age, and in any case of little relevance to the main theme. Ferdinand's rages and remorse make their impact as a perversion of natural affection by deep-seated prejudices of rank and blood which, like the antipathies of race and class in our own society, need only factitious pretexts to erupt into savage violence. His hatred is less controlled than the Cardinal's, but both men are governed by the same murderous enmity. In Bosola's words:

> Your brother and yourself are worthy men;
> You have a pair of hearts like hollow graves,
> Rotten, and rotting others; and your vengeance
> Like two chained bullets, still goes arm in arm...
>
> (IV.ii.18–21)

The Duchess of Malfi takes as its main concern not a panorama of society nor the individual subconscious, but the effects of power upon the human heart and mind. The time-span of the play allows for growth and development in the characters. The Duchess herself matures from act to act; as her hair turns grey the wit and charm of her youth change to gravity and composure. To her love of Antonio is added affectionate care for her children and a deepening religious faith. When the time comes for her to face her brothers' vengeance, she is immune to physical fear and mental torture. It is in keeping with the play's central theme that the revengers should jeer at her marriage and assault her sanity by surrounding her with demented specimens of their corrupt world – mad lawyer, secular priest, jealous doctor, false astrologer, and the like –and follow this by Bosola's attempts to undermine her belief in human dignity. The reply, 'I am Duchess of Malfi still', is an affirmation of reason and an assertion of the Stoic kingship of the mind, undismayed by tyranny. Antonio's premonitions of great men's madness have materialized, but failed in their effect upon a woman whose greatness lies not in rank but natural nobility. With suitable irony, the madness rebounds upon Ferdinand and is incipiently present in the Cardinal. Ferdinand's lycanthropia – his delusion that he is a wolf – results from the murder of his humanity and reduces him to the level of a predatory beast. The darkness of his deed is expressed in the shadow his own shape casts on the ground, which in his insanity he tries to throttle. The Cardinal's guilt likewise projects the hallucination of 'a thing arm'd with a rake'. Both men have poisoned the springs of reason and natural affection, to gain only death and oblivion. The Cardinal dies begging to be 'laid by and never thought of'. Antonio's honest friend Delio speaks the epitaph of these heads of church and state:

> These wretched eminent things
> Leave no more fame behind 'em than should one
> Fall in a frost, and leave his print in snow;
> As soon as the sun shines, it ever melts,
> Both form and matter. (V.v.113–17)[13]

Between the darkness of Duke and Cardinal, and the Duchess who 'lights the time to come', stands Bosola, the unwilling 'slave of power', the would-be ally of its victims. Last in the line of malcontent go-betweens reaching from Malevole to Vindice to Flamineo, he is also the most complex. Already at the beginning of the play his cynicism is changing to disgust. Having suffered seven years in the galleys for a murder suborned by the Cardinal, he is embittered, yet unable to alter his way of life. Bribed to serve again as a spy on the Duchess, he offers to return Ferdinand's gold, but soon accepts his new employment. His genuine admiration for Antonio moves the Duchess to reveal her secret marriage; yet this is a piece of information so valuable that he cannot resist the urge to disclose it and betray her. With the death of the Duchess and the end of his assignment Bosola seeks at once the reward for his crime and some opportunity to atone for it by saving Antonio. He obtains neither; but in his death he at least succeeds in killing those responsible for his own corruption. Neither villain nor hero, Bosola typifies the plight of the intellectual in the world of state, at once its agent and its victim.

The last of the great Jacobean tragedies of state, *The Duchess of Malfi* achieves a tenuous balance between facile optimism and total despair. The good perish with the bad; but human dignity is affirmed; not only in precept, but in character and action. Moreover, the choices that face man in the political world are clearly defined. The corruption of power brings with it madness, sterility and death. In juxtaposition to these, the stand of the Duchess and Antonio becomes identified with reason, fertility, and life. Whether the cosmos is governed by a beneficent heaven or the blind malevolence of the stars; whether the echo of the Duchess's voice telling Antonio he will never see her more alludes to this world or a world to come, is left an open question. But the play's ending suggests more than a merely conventional restoration of order. The young Giovanni who punished Francisco's hired murderers at the end of *The White Devil* may well grow up to become a replica of his uncle, Francisco himself. But the boy standing beside Delio in the closing scene of *The Duchess of Malfi* is Antonio's first-born son, and offers hope of bringing to pass that reformed order his father had longed for in the first scene of the play. In spite of the dread horoscope, despite the opposition of the stars, he has survived. It is arguable, indeed, that this survival was merely due to an oversight in Webster's planning; but a more positive significance cannot be entirely ruled out. A favourite Renaissance maxim declared that reason, or the wise man, overcomes the stars. The unnamed boy standing next to his father's trusted friend may perhaps be taken as a sign, however tenuous, of Webster's trust in the final triumph of reason and his ultimate belief in a better age.

NOTES

1. For a comprehensive account, see Gunnar Boklund, *The Sources of 'The White Devil'* (1957).
2. T. S. Eliot, *Selected Essays* (1951), p. 117.
3. Ian Jack, 'The Case of John Webster', *Scrutiny* XVI (1949), pp. 39–40.
4. John Webster, *The White Devil*, ed. J. R. Brown, The Revels Plays (1960), p. xliv.
5. The parallel situations of Caesar–Antony–Octavia and Francisco–Bracciano–Isabella should be noticed. Isabella's character, her ill-judged journey to Rome, her futile hope to 'work peace' between her husband

and her brother, recall Octavia. In the scene where she appears, the deliberate awkwardness of Caesar's first encounter with Antony is repeated at the meeting of Francisco with Bracciano:

CAESAR: Welcome to Rome.
ANTONY: Thank you.
CAESAR: Sit.
ANTONY: Sit, sir.   (*Antony and Cleopatra*, II.ii.28–31)
                    Enter Bracciano and Flamineo.
FRANCISCO: You are welcome: will you sit ?   (*The White Devil*, II.i.20)
Caesar's accusations of Antony are also paralleled in Monticelso's rebuke of Bracciano, delivered on behalf of Francisco.

CAESAR: Let's grant it is not
                Amiss to tumble on the bed of Ptolemy,
                To give a kingdom for a mirth, to sit
                And keep the turn of tippling with a slave . . .
                        (*Antony and Cleopatra*, I.iv.16–19)
MONTICELSO: It is a wonder to your noble friends
                That you . . .
                Neglect your awful throne, for the soft down
                Of an insatiate bed. O my lord,
                The drunkard after all his lavish cups
                Is dry . . .
                        (*The White Devil*, II.i.26–7, 31–4)

Note how Webster's metaphor of the drunkard takes up the direct reference to drunkenness in Caesar's speech.

6. John Webster, *The Duchess of Malfi*, ed. J. R. Brown, The Revels Plays (1964) p. xxxix. See also Akrigg, p. 227.

7. Antonio is of course biased in the Duchess's favour; but at this point in the play no one knows that he is in love with her, and his words have an effect of chorle objectivity.

8. The case was put tentatively by Clifford Leech, *John Webster* (1951), pp. 68–77, who pointed out that the remarriage of widows, though quite lawful, was viewed with scepticism or disapproval. Chapman's comedy *The Widow's Tears*, and Jeremy Taylor's strictures in *Holy Living*, were cited. (This of course has nothing to do with arguments based on 'order and degree', and depends on attitudes to the individual: stepmothers too are unpopular figures, though Phaedra was a tragic heroine.) Leech nevertheless observed that, as compared with the Cardinal and Ferdinand, 'the Duchess does seem virtue itself', and that 'her revolt against the nature of things seems justified' (pp. 78–9). Inga-Stina Ekeblad repeated Leech's negative arguments, and mentioned Painter's account purporting to show the Duchess as 'an *exemplum horrendum* to all women contemplating a second marriage', in 'The "Impure Art" of John Webster', *Review of*

English Studies n.s. IX (1958), p. 260 (reprinted in *Elizabethan Drama*, ed. Kaufmann, pp. 257–8). Finally in James L. Calderwood's article '*The Duchess of Malfi*: Styles of Ceremony', *Essays in Criticism* 12 (1962), pp. 133–47, opinion hardens into dogma. The Duchess is punished for her 'uninhibited passion', her 'violation of Degree', and her 'disrespect for external realities'.

9. William Painter, *The Palace of Pleasure* (1567) vol. ii, nov. xxii, reprinted in *The Duchess of Malfi*, ed. J. R. Brown, p. 179.

10. *The Duchess of Malfi*, ed. J. R. Brown, pp. 183–4.

11. On this practice see J. W. Saunders, 'The Facade of Morality', in *That Soueraine Light: Essays in Honor of Edmund Spenser* 1552–92, ed. William R. Mueller and Don Cameron Allen (1952), pp. 6–7, and Paul Siegel, 'Christianity and the Religion of Love', *Shakespeare Quarterly* XII (1961), pp. 371–2.

12. Marriage in the presence of a witness was valid by canon law and English common law when consent was expressed *per verba de praesenti*, 'in words of the present'; see Ernest Schanzer, 'The Marriage-Contracts in *Measure for Measure*', *Shakespeare Survey* 13 (1960), pp. 81–9. In Catholic countries such marriages were forbidden in the mid-sixteenth century by the Council of Trent, but its jurisdiction was not of course recognized by the Church of England, and Protestant audiences would see nothing inherently sinful in the Duchess's marriage to Antonio. Her remark,

> How can the church bind faster?
> We now are man and wife, and 'tis the church
> That must but echo this.   (I.i.491–3)

would be a normal English comment. The marriage should have been later solemnized; whether or not this took place we are not told in the play; but when Ferdinand calls her children bastards according to 'our national law', the Duchess replies 'You violate a sacrament o' the church' (IV.i.39).

13. Cf. *Sejanus* V. 893–7:

> Forbear, you things,
> That stand upon the pinnacles of state,
> To boast your slippery height. When you do fall,
> You pash yourselves in pieces, ne'er to rise,
> And he that lends you pity is not wise.

Index

Index